# JUSTIFICATION

# JUSTIFICATION

## FRANCIS TURRETIN

TRANSLATED BY GEORGE MUSGRAVE GIGER

EDITED BY JAMES T. DENNISON JR.

INTRODUCTION BY R. C. SPROUL

**Sixteenth Topic of**
*Institutes of Elenctic Theology*

P U B L I S H I N G
P.O. BOX 817 • PHILLIPSBURG • NEW JERSEY 08865-0817

*Page design and typesetting by Lakeside Design Plus*

Printed in the United States of America

**Library of Congress Cataloging-in-Publication Data**

Turrettini, François, 1623–1687.
    [Institutio theologiae elencticae. English]
    Justification / Francis Turretin ; translated by George Musgrave Giger ; edited by James T. Dennison, Jr., ; introduction by R.C. Sproul.
        p. cm.
    Previously published in vol. 2 of Institutes of elenctic theology. c1992–c1997.
    Includes bibliographical references and index. ISBN 0-87552-705-1 (pbk.)
    1. Reformed Church—Doctrines—Early works to 1800.
    2. Theology, Doctrinal—Early works to 1800. 3. Catholic Church—Controversial literature—Early works to 1800. I. Giger, George Musgrave. II. Dennison, James T., 1943- III. Title.
BX9422.3.T8713 2004
234'.7—dc22

2003065952

# CONTENTS

# INTRODUCTION

R. C. SPROUL

*"Articulus stantis et cadentis ecclesiae."* These words, perhaps arcane to the modern reader, announce boldly Martin Luther's assessment of the importance of the doctrine of justification by faith alone. His assessment speaks to not an abstract point of doctrine but to the very life of the church. Here Luther calls justification "the article upon which the church stands or falls." For him the issue of justification touches not merely the church's "well-being" (*bene esse*), but the church's very essence or being (*esse*). Without this doctrine the church falls; she collapses into ruin. She ceases to be a true church. Though every other article of historic Christian faith remains intact—if this one (*sola fide*) is lost, the church is lost with it.

Elsewhere Luther continues to insist that this doctrine was of paramount importance, essential to the gospel itself. Some of his further assertions include:

> This doctrine is the head and the cornerstone. It alone begets, nourishes, builds, preserves, and defends the church of God; and without it the church of God cannot exist for one hour. . . .[1]

1. Martin Luther, *What Luther Says: An Anthology*, 3 vols., ed. Ewald M. Plass (St. Louis: Concordia, 1959), 2:704.

Whoever departs from the article of justification does not
know God and is an idolater. . . . For when this article has
been taken away, nothing remains but error, hypocrisy, god-
lessness, and idolatry, although it may seem to be the height
of truth, worship of God, holiness, etc.[2]

Again:

The article of justification is the master and prince, the lord,
the ruler, and the judge over all kinds of doctrines; it pre-
serves and governs all church doctrine and raises up our conscience before God. Without this article the world is utter
death and darkness.[3]

Luther's stress on the supreme importance of justification
may be seen as a mere exercise in hyperbole, or the result of
the anguish he suffered before discovering *sola fide*, or even
the torment he endured in the subsequent controversy regarding it. Some dismiss his strong statements as mere bom-
bast, emotional utterances not rooted in sober analysis.

Luther sought to give a reason for elevating *sola fide* to the
level of supremacy among Christian doctrines. He explains:

If the article of justification is lost, all Christian doctrine is
lost at the same time. And all the people in the world who
do not hold to this justification are either Jews or Turks or
papists or heretics; for there is no middle ground between
these two righteousnesses: the active one of the Law and the
passive one which comes from Christ. Therefore the man
who strays from Christian righteousness must relapse into
the active one, that is, since he has lost Christ he must put his
confidence in his own works.[4]

2. *Ibid.*
3. *Ibid.*, 703.
4. *Ibid.*

Here we see the crux of the matter for Luther. He views *sola fide* as inseparably tied to (1) the gospel and (2) the redeeming work of Christ. To reject *sola fide* is to reject the gospel itself and to rob Christ of his imputed righteousness as the sole ground of our justification.

Luther is not alone in his assessment of the central importance of justification. Calvin expresses a similar sentiment. He calls justification the "hinge" upon which everything turns:

> The doctrine of justification . . . is the principal ground on which religion must be supported, so it requires greater care and attention. For unless you understand first of all what your position is before God, and what the judgment [is] which he passes upon you, you have no foundation on which your salvation can be laid, or on which piety towards God can be reared.[5]

We note in passing that both Luther and Calvin use the metaphor of a "foundation" to show how basic *sola fide* is to the Christian faith and how much else relies on it for their support.

The stress on the essential importance of *sola fide* in the sixteenth century has been weakened in modern time. In his comprehensive treatment of the doctrine of justification, Alister McGrath writes:

> On the basis of the above analysis, it will be clear that there exist real differences between Protestants and Roman Catholics over the matter of justification. *The question remains, however, as to the significance of these differences.* How important, for example, is the distinction between an alien and an intrinsic justifying righteousness? In recent years, there appears to be an increasing sympathy for the view that these differences,

5. John Calvin, *Institutes of the Christian Religion*, 2 vols., trans. Henry Beveridge (1845; repr., Grand Rapids: Eerdmans, 1964), 2:37 (3.11.1).

although of importance in the Reformation period, no longer possess the significance that they once had. . . . It seems that in the modern period the Christian denominations have preferred to concentrate on their points of agreement, rather than draw attention to their historical disagreements! ——

This may be due in part to an increasing recognition that today the real threat to the Gospel of grace comes from the rationalism of the Enlightenment rather than from other Christian denominations.[6]

What? The "real" threat to the gospel is the rationalism of the Enlightenment? Was the Roman view of justification by inherent righteousness only a chimera? Was Paul shadowboxing with the Judaizers of Galatia? Is it now permissible to accept another gospel that we may be unified against rationalism?

"How important," McGrath asks, "is the distinction between an alien and an intrinsic justifying righteousness?"

Let Luther answer McGrath's question:

A Christian is righteous and holy by an alien or foreign holiness—I call it this for the sake of instruction—that is, he is righteous by the mercy and grace of God. . . . It is a divine blessing, given us through the true knowledge of the Gospel, when we know or believe that our sin has been forgiven through the grace and merit of Christ. . . . Is not this righteousness an alien righteousness? It consists completely in the indulgence of another and is a pure gift of God, who shows mercy and favor for Christ's sake.[7]

For Luther the essence of the gospel—the good news of the gospel—is that the merit and righteousness we need to be jus-

6. Alister E. McGrath, *Iustitia Dei: A History of the Christian Doctrine of Justification,* 2 vols. (Cambridge: Cambridge U. P., 1986), 1:9.

7. Luther, *What Luther Says,* 710–11.

tified is not found in us, even by the help of grace. It is found apart from us—it is a righteousness *extra nos*—a righteousness that properly belongs to Christ himself—which righteousness is imputed to me by faith. Take away that imputation and you leave me helpless in my sin.

I see nothing unique about the sinner's condition before the throne of God's judgment in sixteenth-century people. I am as desperate in my need for an alien righteousness as Luther was. Nothing in the course of history has rendered the distinction between an alien and an intrinsic justifying righteousness unimportant or less important. If McGrath and others believe that distinction is now not so significant, let them confess their own sins. If McGrath thinks he can stand before God without an alien righteousness imputed to him, let him take the dare. For me, without the imputation of an alien righteousness I have no hope in this life or the next.

When the crucial importance of *sola fide* fades in the judgment of men, it indicates a new eclipse of the gospel itself.

I hear the banter, "Justification by faith alone was important in the sixteenth century, but not now." Or, "It was all a misunderstanding, a tempest in a teapot. Now we can all get along without resolving the issue." Such sentiment is like the medicine of the false prophets of Israel whose cries of " 'peace, peace!' when there is no peace," only served to "heal the wounds of the daughter of Zion slightly."

In one sense McGrath was prophetic. Almost before the ink was dry on his book, the evangelical world was rocked by two internal controversies regarding justification. First was the so-called lordship-salvation debate that broke out among the dispensationalists. The two camps engaged in sharp polemics over the relationship between faith and works.

Soon after, the initiative "Evangelicals and Catholics Together" (ECT) provoked a firestorm over claims of unity in the gospel between Roman Catholics committed to Catholic orthodoxy and professed Evangelical leaders.

The involvement of J. I. Packer in the ECT initiative was puzzling to many. In his introductory essay to the reprint of James Buchanan's classic work on justification, Packer wrote:

> For the doctrine of justification by faith is like Atlas: it bears a world on its shoulders, the entire evangelical knowledge of saving grace. The doctrines of election, of effectual calling, regeneration, and repentance, of adoption, of prayer, of the church, the ministry, and the sacraments, have all to be interpreted and understood in the light of justification by faith. . . . when justification falls, all true knowledge of the grace of God in human life falls with it, and then, as Luther said, the church itself falls. . . . When Atlas falls, everything that rested on his shoulders comes crashing down too.[8]

Between the writing of this essay and the appearance of ECT, something happened. When pressed by friends and followers as to why he signed ECT, Packer responded in Christianity Today with "Why I Signed It."[9] He refers to *sola fide* as the "small print" of the gospel. The metaphor of Atlas gave way to the metaphor of small print. James Montgomery Boice debated Packer behind closed doors in San Antonio, where Boice insisted that *sola fide* is the "bold print" of the gospel. Somewhere between the reprinting of Buchanan's classic and the appearance of ECT, Atlas shrugged.

In addition to the controversies provoked by the "lordship-salvation" question and the ECT initiative, we have also seen serious questions raised within the Christian academic com-

---

8. J. I. Packer, "Introductory Essay," in James Buchanan, *The Doctrine of Justification: An Outline of Its History in the Church, and of Its Exposition from Scripture* (1867; repr., London: Banner of Truth, 1961), Bt764 .B8.

9. J. I. Packer, "Why I Signed It," *Christianity Today* 38 (December 1994): 34–37.

munity, particularly with respect to the concept of imputation. The so-called "New Perspective on Paul" has inclined some scholars to embrace a shift in the understanding of the New Testament concept of justification. Paul is seen as teaching not so much an individualistic notion of personal justification (in a legal sense), but of speaking of the change of a person's status with respect to the covenant community.

The "New Perspective" has led some to conclude that the historic conflict between Rome and the Reformers was a case of *false dilemma*, in which the either/or fallacy was committed. That is, *both* sides erred in their understanding of the Biblical view of justification. Thus a pox is declared on both houses.

The controversy at Westminster Theological Seminary in Philadelphia over theologian Norman Shepherd's teaching regarding justification remains unresolved. The number of Shepherd's followers has increased over the years since he was dismissed from Westminster.

With all these contemporary debates regarding aspects of the Reformation doctrine of justification, it is a welcome relief for Francis Turretin's work on the subject to appear in this special volume drawn from his larger work, *Institutes of Elenctic Theology*.[10] Turretin represents the teaching of the high age of the Protestant Scholasticism in the seventeenth century.

In our day mention of Scholasticism, whether Roman Catholic or Protestant, is greeted by a curled lip and a snarl. Our culture, so heavily influenced by the categories of existential philosophy, has a palpable animus toward all things rational. That theology might be carried out in a rigorous

---

10. Francis Turretin, *Institutes of Elenctic Theology*, 3 vols., trans. George Musgrave Giger, ed. James T. Dennison Jr. (Phillipsburg, N.J.: P&R, 1994).

logical style seems almost irreligious and unspiritual. Thinking gives way to feeling and clarity gives way to confusion. Known as "The Age of Reason," the seventeenth century featured rationalist philosophers (such as Descartes, Malebranche, Leibniz, and Spinoza) who stressed the priority of the deductive over the inductive, the logical over the empirical.

Philosophical movements tend to influence how theology is done or is expressed in any given time period, and Turretin's style is no exception. His approach to theological issues seems almost geometric; he develops proofs for his theorems in an acutely logical fashion.

Often the contrast between sixteenth-century Reformation theology and seventeenth-century theology is painted as a contrast between original creative insight and rigid codification. The charge of reification is leveled against Turretin and his contemporaries. That is, he is accused of turning the living faith of the sixteenth century into a stone-like cold abstract series of orthodox formulae.

These charges, however, reveal much more of our own era than they do of Turretin's. They tend to be made by people who are allergic to intellectual precision and prefer the comfort zone of ambiguity. But if we hold sacred the notion that God has created us with minds for the purpose of seeking understanding, then we will delight in the clarity and precision of thought Turretin's work presents to us.

C. Matthew McMahon says of Turretin:

> Among Reformed Theologians of the world, both present and past, Francis Turretin's *Institutio* fares among the greatest Protestant theological work ever written. And if more disciples of Jesus Christ were to pick this work up and read it, then live it, the church would [be] a force to be reckoned with in this 21st century. We may compare Turretin's work against Luther's voluminous productions, Calvin's writings,

and others. Yet, I believe Turretin's theological compilation and sheer depth outweighs them all. Some may disagree knowing Calvin and Luther, and others, were the foundations on which Turretin's biblical theology emerged, and this may be true, yet his logic, order, and keen insight into the Scriptures shine brighter among the scholastics than any I know.[11]

Just as the most acute Roman Catholic scholastic, Thomas Aquinas, stood on the shoulders of his predecessors (especially Augustine), so Turretin was conscious that he stood on the shoulders of titans that came before him such as Calvin and Theodore Beza.

In the summer of 2002 I was visiting the old city of Geneva, Switzerland. I had taken a tour group to see St. Peter's, John Calvin's church. As we moved from the church down to Reformation Park to view the Reformation Wall, we paused for a few minutes on a bridge behind the Geneva Academy. I was awed by how much spiritual influence spread from this small building to reach around the world. The Academy was founded in 1559, completed in 1564. The original building, with Theodore Beza as its first rector, still stands today.

Even before the formal establishment of the Academy, Calvin's teaching drew refugees from Europe and Great Britain to Geneva. Here the Scottish Reformer John Knox was trained in the Reformed faith. Here refugees came from England to escape the persecution of Mary Tudor ("Bloody Mary"), who reigned from 1553 to 1558. During this time the British refugees in Geneva worked under Calvin's tutelage to produce the Geneva Bible. Published in 1560, this Bible dominated the English-speaking world for a hundred years

11. C. Matthew McMahon, "Francis Turretin," *A Puritan's Mind,* http://www.apuritansmind.com/FrancisTurretin/francisturretin.htm.

before the King James Bible supplanted it. The Geneva Bible was the Bible of Shakespeare, of the Puritans, and of the Pilgrims who brought it to the shores of the New World.

Here, in this Genevan tradition, Francis Turretin flourished as a teacher of theology.

An American adage, "You can't make a silk purse from a sow's ear" can in the case of the Turretin family be refashioned: "You can make great theologians from purses filled from silk." The Turretin family had its roots in Italy's Tuscany region, where they had a heavy interest in the silk trade in and around the city of Lucca. In the sixteenth century Regolo Turretin became the chief magistrate of Lucca.

In 1541 the Reformation came to Lucca in the person of Peter Martyr Vermigli. After a brief sojourn there, he was forced to flee the Inquisition in 1542, but not before the seed of Reformation was planted. The first of the Turretins to embrace the Reformed faith was Regolo's son, Francis. Because of his conversion he fled Italy and eventually settled in Geneva. Francis maintained a flourishing silk business there and was a key figure in the financial community of Geneva.

Francis' son Benedict was a student at the Geneva Academy, studying under Theodore Beza and Jean Deodati. In 1611 he was appointed to the faculty of the Academy where he became professor of theology. His career was stellar but short—he died in 1631. Benedict's third child was a gifted boy born in 1623, named for his grandfather, and author of this work on justification.

As a young student Francis studied both philosophy and theology at the Academy. From Geneva he went to Holland and enrolled at Leyden. He then studied further in France, both in Paris and Saumur (where he was exposed to Amyrauld, whose teachings he contested.)

## PRINCETON SCHOOL

In 1648 Francis returned to Geneva to pastor the church of Geneva. He preached regularly to a large group of Italian refugees, with great impact. The Academy persistently called him to teach philosophy there, but he declined in order to follow his pastoral vocation. He later returned to Holland where he filled a Leyden pulpit.

In 1653 the call came again with greater urgency for Francis to return to Geneva, to replace his former mentor as Chair of Theology. This time he assented, joining the Academy's faculty and resuming his duties as pastor of the Italian church. He continued in both positions until his death in 1687.

Turretin's contemporaries celebrated not only his erudition but also praised his eloquence and his ministries of mercy—to the poor, to orphans, to widows. His pastor's heart made him an evangelist who pled with sinners, with tears, to be reconciled with God. He also excelled in statesmanship in the Reformation countries of his time.

Perhaps Turretin's greatest strength was his acute intellect. He was a master of precision, of fine distinctions. The precision in turn yields lucidity by which the understanding is enriched. He embodied the ancient adage: *pi bene distinquit, bene docet.* (Who distinguishes well, teaches well.)

Turretin's thirst for precision was consistent with the spirit of Geneva's most famous resident, John Calvin. Calvin had little time for theological games in which the "studied ambiguity" was a standard play. The studied ambiguity is an intentional ambiguity by which words and phrases are left blurry enough for antithetical views to be safely held by both sides in a debate.

For example, people try to transcend the issue of justification that separates Roman Catholics and Protestants by saying, "We believe that we are justified by the righteousness of Christ." Both sides can agree on this formulation while at the same time understanding it radically differently. By the righteousness of Christ, Rome means the *infusion* of Christ's righteousness into the believer which when co-operated with assists a person to become actually righteous. The Protestant understands the formula to refer to the *imputation* of the righteousness of Christ to the account of the believer. The difference between these two is the essence of the Reformation debate, then and now.

Speaking with respect to historic language and formulations of the doctrine of the Trinity and those who engaged in the art of logomachy, Calvin said:

> Such novelty (if novelty it should be called) becomes most requisite, when the truth is to be maintained against calumniators who evade it by quibbling. Of this, we of the present day have too much experience in being constantly called upon to attack the enemies of pure and sound doctrine. These slippery snakes escape by their swift and tortuous windings, if not strenuously pursued, and when caught, firmly held. Thus the early Christians, when harassed with the disputes which heresies produced, were forced to declare their sentiments in terms most scrupulously exact in order that no indirect subterfuges might remain to ungodly men, to whom ambiguity of expression was a kind of hiding-place.[12]

Church history testifies that the studied ambiguity is the refuge of the heretic. If he can blur his meaning, he can safely continue to slither along on his belly.

A revival of interest in the work of Turretin occurred in the nineteenth century among theologians who also sought precision in theological formulations. This was so at "Old Princeton" when the Princeton theologians, most notably

---

12. John Calvin, *Institutes*, 1:111–12 (1.13.4).

Charles Hodge, relied heavily upon Turretin. It was at Hodge's request that George Musgrave Giger prepared an English translation of Turretin.[13] Robert Dabney of the Southern Presbyterian Church, W. G. T. Shedd of Union, New York, and William Cunningham of New College, Edinburgh, also drew on Turretin.[14]

## THE PRESENT VOLUME

In this volume *Justification*, taken from *Institutes of Elenctic Theology*, Turretin plunges right into the Biblical meaning of the term *justification*, arguing that the chief meaning of the term is forensic in character. That is, justification refers to a legal declaration made by God. It is not to be confused with a moral process that takes place within the life of the believer, which the Bible calls sanctification. At the core of the Reformation debate with Rome was a confusion between sanctification and justification. Luther's maxim *simul justus et peccator* captured the Protestant view that in our justification we are pronounced just (forensically), while in ourselves we are still sinners. Though sanctification begins immediately at justification, our justification does not depend upon a prior sanctification.

In a different sense Rome has her own sort of "forensic" justification: justification occurs when God pronounces a person just. The difference is that for Rome God's forensic declaration is based upon God's divine analysis of the moral state of the believer. If a person is truly just inherently, then, and only then, will God pronounce him just. The Protestant view of forensic justification involves God's declaring a per-

13. Turretin, *Institutes*, vol. III, *The Life and Career of Francis Turretin*, by James T. Dennison Jr., 648.
14. *Ibid.*

son just on the grounds of the imputation of Christ's righteousness to him.

This crucial difference is described by the terms *analytical* and *synthetic* justification. Analytical justification describes the Roman Catholic view. In this schema God "forensically" declares a person just when, under divine analysis a person is seen to be inherently just. To be inherently just is to have righteousness and/or justness in oneself. This inherent justice may not be *by* oneself, but it must nevertheless be *in* oneself. One does not achieve this righteousness by the unaided activity of the self. Rome is not Pelagian in its view of justification. (Pelagius taught that a person can become perfectly righteous without the aid of divine grace. For him, grace "facilitates" righteousness but is not a necessary condition for attaining it.)

According to Rome the inherent righteousness necessary for justification is attained only by the assistance of the infused grace of Christ. The believer, however, must co-operate with (*cooperare*) and assent to (*assentire*) this grace. Thus synergistically the believer can become righteous in himself, though it is not by himself as it requires the assistance of grace.

Once righteousness truly inheres in a person, then the judgment of God that the person is just is analytical. God declares the person just because the person actually *is* just. Here we see how in the Roman view justification is the consequence of sanctification, not its impetus.

In linguistic philosophy an analytical statement is basically a tautology, a statement that is true by definition (or by analysis). In such statements there is nothing in the predicate that is not already inherent in the subject. A statement like "A triangle has three angles" or "A bachelor is an unmarried man" is analytical because nothing new is added in the predicate.

Synthetic statements add something in the predicate that is not in the subject. The predicate carries a certain plus. If we say "The bachelor is rich" we are asserting something about a particular bachelor that is not universal to bachelorhood. Here we have a *synthesis* of two concepts: bachelorhood and wealth.

The difference between analytical and synthetic justification is all the difference in the world. It is not a mere abstraction or nominal sense of words. In analytical justification God only justifies those who are already just. They may have been formerly unjust but the declaration of justification can only come after the sinner becomes truly just. This is rooted unfortunately in the Latin term for justification, *iustificare*, which means literally "to make just."

The Reformation view of synthetic justification stands in stark and radical contrast to the analytical view of Rome. In this view God's legal (forensic) declaration by which the sinner is reckoned or counted righteous is based upon something that is *added* to the person. That which is added by imputation is the righteousness of Christ. This is the essence of what Luther was declaring in his formula *simul justus et peccator*. We are at the same time just and sinner. We are just by imputation (synthetically) while we are still sinners inherently (analytically).

This distinction launched Rome's counter-protest to the Protestant Reformation. She argues that the Reformation view makes God a liar, involving him in a "legal fiction." The fiction is that God is involved in a forensic (legal) declaration by which he declares a person to be just when the person, in fact, is not just. This involves fiction, not reality.

This objection (as I have discussed elsewhere[15]) misses the very heart and soul of the gospel and reveals Rome's

---

15. See R. C. Sproul, *Faith Alone: The Evangelical Doctrine of Justification*, (Grand Rapids: Baker, 1995), 105–8.

rejection of that gospel. If her argument were sound, it would prove too much. It would negate the atonement itself since the atonement rests upon the concept of imputation. Christ bears our sins via imputation. If imputation necessitates a legal fiction, then the cross would also be a legal fiction and each person would have to atone for his or her own sins.

But the gospel is no fiction. It announces a profound reality that while we are still sinners, Christ justifies us. We are counted or reckoned to be righteous because there is a real (not fictional) imputation of the real (not fictional) righteousness of Christ to our account.

That Rome's view is analytical may be seen in her response to the Reformation doctrine in the Counter Reformation Council of Trent. In the sixteenth chapter of the Sixth Session of Trent we read:

> Thus, neither is our own justice established as our own from ourselves (Rom. 10:3; 2 Cor. 3:5), nor is the justice of God ignored or repudiated, for that justice which is called ours, because we are justified by its inherence in us, that same is (the justice) of God, because it is infused into us by God through us by God through the merit of Christ.[16]

This is the issue, the ground of our justification. Is it the righteousness of Christ *in* us or the righteousness of Christ *for* us?

Turretin is at his best when he addresses this issue. He demolishes the claim of inherent righteousness, showing that it cannot justify us simply because we never truly attain it in this life. What works we do perform are excluded from our justification. Turretin lists several arguments against this

---

16. *Canons and Decrees of the Council of Trent: Original Text with English Translation*, trans. H. J. Schroeder (London: Herder, 1941), 41.

view but the most telling is that we remain tainted by imperfection through this life.

We see why the Roman Catholic Church constructed her
artificial doctrine of purgatory. For the Roman church, no
one is justified without purgatory (except in the rare case of
isolated saints). All who die with impurities (which we
would say includes all who die) must have those impurities
"purged" before they are fit for heaven.

How far has the gospel been removed? If I must wait until I become inherently righteous in order to be justified, I
must wait forever. Gone is my assurance. Gone is the joy of
my salvation. Gone is my remission of sins. Gone is my
adoption into the family of God. Gone is the cloak of the
righteousness of Christ that covers my filthy garments.

Who will rescue me from sin and death? Rome provides
her answer: the Church. It is the church that has the power
of the keys. The church possesses the treasury of merit
wherein my impurities may be cured by the saints (but not
by the imputation of the merit of Christ).

The difference between infusion and imputation is not a
matter of semantics. It is not a tempest in a teapot. It is not
a simple dispute between two words. No, the difference is
systemic. The entire Roman Catholic structure of salvation
is utterly incompatible with the biblical gospel. No one
shows this more clearly than Francis Turretin.

# Ten Questions

1. Is the word *justification* always used in a forensic sense in this argument; or is it also used in a moral and physical sense? The former we affirm; the latter we deny against the Romanists.

2. Is the impulsive and meritorious cause (on account of which man is justified in the judgment of God) inherent righteousness infused into us or good works? We deny against the Romanists.

3. Is the righteousness and obedience of Christ imputed to us the meritorious cause and foundation of our justification with God? We affirm against the Romanists and Socinians.

4. Does justification consist only in the remission of sins? Or does it embrace also adoption and the right to life? The former we deny and affirm the latter.

5. Does remission of sins consist in an absolute removal of them? Or in the pardon of them? And after the guilt is remitted is a certain punishment retained? Or is it wholly remitted? The former we deny; the latter we affirm against the Romanists.

6. What is the adoption which is given to us in justification?

7. Does faith justify us properly and of itself or only relatively and instrumentally? The former we deny; the latter we affirm against the Socinians, Remonstrants and Romanists.

8. Does faith alone justify? We affirm against the Romanists.

9. Was justification made from eternity or is it made in time? Is it an undivided act taking place at one and the same time?

10. The unity, perfection and certainty of justification.

# THE WORD
# *JUSTIFICATION*

*Is the word* justification *always used in a forensic sense in this argument; or is it also used in a moral and physical sense? The former we affirm; the latter we deny against the Romanists.*

As in the chain of salvation justification follows calling (Rom. 8:30) and is everywhere set forth as the primary effect of faith, the topic concerning calling and faith begets the topic concerning justification. This must be handled with the greater care and accuracy as this saving doctrine is of the greatest importance in religion. It is called by Luther "the article of a standing and a falling church." By other Christians, it is termed the characteristic and basis of Christianity—not without reason—the principal rampart of the Christian religion. This being adulterated or subverted, it is impossible to retain purity of doctrine in other places. Hence Satan in every way has endeavored to corrupt this doctrine in all ages, as has been done especially in the papacy. For this reason, it is deservedly placed among the primary causes of our secession from the Roman church and of the Reformation.

However, although some of the more candid Romanists (conquered by the force of the truth) have felt and expressed themselves more soundly than others concerning this article (nor are there wanting also some among other divines who, influenced by a desire to lessen controversies, think there is not so great matter for dispute about it and that there are here not a few logomachies), still it is certain that up to this time there are between us and the Romanists in this argument controversies not only verbal, but real and many which are of great importance (as will be made manifest in what follows).

From a false and preposterous explanation of the word, the truth of the thing itself has been wonderfully obscured. In the first place, its genuine sense (and in this question most especially) must be unfolded. This being settled, we will be able the more easily to reach the nature of the thing itself.

The word *htsdyq*, to which the Greek *dikaioun* answers and the Latin *justificare*, is used in two ways in the Scriptures—properly and improperly. Properly the verb is forensic, put for "to absolve" anyone in a trial or "to hold" and to declare "just"; as opposed to the verb "to condemn" and "to accuse" (Ex. 23:7; Deut. 25:1; Prov. 17:15; Luke 18:14; Rom. 3–5). Thus apart from a trial, it is used to acknowledge and to praise one as just and that too either deservedly (as when it is terminated on God, in which way men are said to justify God when they celebrate him as just [Ps. 51:4]; "wisdom" is said to be "justified of her children" [Matt. 11:19; Luke 7:35], i.e., acknowledged and celebrated as such); or presumptuously ([*doxastōs*] as the Pharisees are said to justify themselves, Luke 16:15). Improperly it is used either ministerially, for to bring to righteousness (Dan. 12:3 where *mtsdyqy* seems to be exegetical of [*exēgētikon tou*] *mskylym* because while the preachers of the gospel instruct and teach believers, by this very thing they justify them ministerially [to wit, by teaching them the true way in which they can be justified] in the same sense in which they are said to save them, 1 Tim. 4:16). Or by way of synecdoche (the antecedent being put for the consequent) for "to free"; "he that is dead is justified from sin" (Rom. 6:7), i.e., freed. Or comparatively, where on account of a comparison between the sins of Israel and Samaria, Israel is said "to justify Samaria" (Ezek. 16:51–52) and the sins of Judah increasing, Judah is said "to have justified Israel" (Jer. 3:11) because Israel was more just than Judah (i.e., her sins were fewer than the sins of Judah).

Hence arises the question with the Romanists concerning the acceptation of this word—whether it is to be taken precisely in a forensic sense in this affair; or whether it ought also to be taken in a physical and moral sense for the infusion of righteousness and justification, if it is allowable (so to speak) either by the acquisition or the increase of it. For they do not deny that the word *justificatio* and the verb *justificare* are often taken in a forensic sense, even in this matter, as Bellarmine, Tirinus, Toletus, and not a few others. Yet they do not wish this to be the constant meaning, but that it often signifies a true production, acquisition or increase of righteousness; this is especially the case when employed about the justification of man before God. Hence they distinguish justification into "first and second." The first is that by which the man who is unjust is made just; the second is that by which a just man is made more just. Hence Bellarmine says: "Justification undoubtedly is a certain movement from sin to righteousness, and takes its name from the terminus to which it leads, as all other similar motions, illumination, calefaction; that is true justification, where some righteousness is acquired beyond the remission of sin." Thomas Aquinas says, "Justification taken passively implies a motion to making righteous, just as calefaction a motion to heat." Now although we do not deny that this word has more than one signification and is taken in different ways in the Scriptures (now properly, then improperly, as we have already said), still we maintain that it is never taken for an infusion of righteousness, but as often as the Scriptures speak professedly about our justification, it always must be explained as a forensic term.

The reasons are: (1) the passages which treat of justification admit to no other than a forensic sense (cf. Job 9:3; Ps. 143:2; Rom. 3:28; 4:1–3; Acts 13:39 and elsewhere). A judicial process is set forth and mention is made of an accusing "law," of "accused persons" who are guilty (*hypodikoi*, Rom. 3:19), of a "hand-writing" contrary to us (Col. 2:14), of divine "justice" demanding punishment (Rom. 3:24, 26), of an "advocate" pleading the cause (1 John 2:1), of "satisfaction" and imputed righteousness (Rom. 4 and 5), of a "throne of grace" before which we are absolved (Heb. 4:16), of a "judge" pronouncing sentence (Rom. 3:20) and absolving sinners (Rom. 4:5).

(2) Justification is opposed to condemnation: "Who shall lay anything to the charge of God's elect? It is God that justifieth. Who is he that condemneth?" (Rom. 8:33–34). As therefore accusation and condemnation occur only in a trial, so also justification. Nor can it be conceived how God can be said to condemn or to justify, unless either by adjudging to punishment or absolving us from it judicially. Toletus is compelled to confess this on Romans 8:33: "The word justification in this place is taken with that signification, which is opposed to its antithesis, namely, condemnation; so that it is the same in this place to justify as to pronounce just, as a judge by his sentence absolves and pronounces innocent." Cornelius a Lapide, who otherwise earnestly strives to obscure the truth, still overcome by the force of the truth, acknowledges that God justifies (i.e., absolves from the threatened action of sin and the Devil and pronounces just).

(3) The equivalent phrases by which our justification is described are judicial: such as "not to come into judgment" (John 5:24), "not to be condemned" (John 3:18), "to remit sins," "to impute righteousness" (Rom. 4), "to be reconciled" (Rom. 5:10; 2 Cor. 5:19) and the like. (4) This word ought to be employed in the sense in which it was used by Paul in his disputation against the Jews. Yet it is certain that he did not speak there of an infusion of righteousness (viz., whether from faith or from the works of the law, the habit of righteousness should be infused into man), but how the sinner could stand before the judgment seat of God and obtain a right to life (whether by the works of the law, as the Jews imagined, or by faith in Christ). And since the thought concerning justification arose without doubt from a fear of divine judgment and of the wrath to come, it cannot be used in any other than a forensic sense (as it was used in the origin of those questions which were agitated in a former age upon the occasion of indulgences, satisfactions and remission of sins). (5) Finally, unless this word is taken in a forensic sense, it would be confounded with sanctification. But that these are distinct, both the nature of the thing and the voice of Scripture frequently prove.

Although the word *justification* in certain passages of Scripture should recede from its proper signification and be taken in another than a forensic sense, it would not follow that it is taken judicially by us falsely because the proper sense is to be looked to in those passages in which the foundation of this doctrine is formed. (2) Although perchance it should not be taken precisely in a forensic sense for "to pronounce just" and "to absolve in a trial," still we maintain that it cannot be taken in a physical sense for the infusion of righteousness, as the Romanists hold (as is easily proved from the passages brought forward by Bellarmine himself).

In Isaiah 53:11, where it is said Christ "by his knowledge shall justify many," it is manifest that reference is made to the meritorious and instrumental cause of our absolution with God (namely, Christ and the knowledge or belief of him). For the knowledge of Christ here ought not to be taken subjectively concerning the knowledge by which he knows what was agreed upon between himself and the Father (which has nothing to do with our justification); but objectively concerning that knowledge by which he is known by his people unto salvation (which is nothing else than faith, to which justification is everywhere ascribed). The following words show no other sense is to be sought when it is added "for he shall bear their iniquities." This denotes the satisfaction of Christ, which faith ought to embrace in order that we may be justified.

Nor does the passage in Daniel 12:3 press us. As we have already said, justification is ascribed to the ministers of the gospel, as elsewhere the salvation of believers is ascribed to them (1 Tim. 4:16; 1 Cor. 9:22). Not assuredly by an infusion of habitual righteousness (which does not come within their power), but by the instruction of believers by which, as they open the way of life, so they teach the mode by which sinners can obtain justification in Christ by faith. Hence the Vulgate does not translate it *justificantes,* but *erudientes ad justitiam.*

"He that is righteous, let him be righteous still" (Rev. 22:11) does not favor our opponents so as to denote an infusion or increase of righteousness. Thus it would be tautological (*tautologia*) with the following words, "He that is holy, let him be holy still," because justification would not differ from sanctification. But it is best to refer it to the application and sense of justification; for although on the part of God justification does not take place successively, still on our part it is apprehended by us by varied and repeated actions, while by new acts of faith we apply to ourselves from time to time the merit of Christ as a remedy for the daily sins into which we fall. Nay, although it should be granted that the exercise of righteousness is here meant (as in a manuscript we have *dikaiosynēn poiēsatō*) that it may be opposed to the preceding words—"He that is unjust, let him be more unjust"—the opinion of the Romanists will not on that account be established.

"The justification of the wicked" of which Paul speaks (Rom. 4:5), ought not to be referred to an infusion or increase of habitual righteousness, but belongs to the remission of sins (as it is explained by the apostle from David). Nay, it would not be a justification of the wicked, if it were used in any other sense than for a judicial absolution at the throne of grace. I confess that God in declaring just ought also for that very reason to make just so that his judgment may be according to truth. But man can be made just in two ways: either in himself or in another; either from the law or from the gospel. God therefore makes him just whom he justifies; not in himself, as if from a sight of his inherent righteousness he declared him just, but from the view of the righteousness imputed—in Christ. It is indeed an abomination to Jehovah to justify the wicked without a due satisfaction, but God in this sense justifies no wicked one (Christ having been given to us as a surety who received upon himself the punishment we deserved).

Although certain words of the same order with justification denote an effecting in the subject, there is not the same reason for this, which otherwise barbarously has been received into Latinity to express the force of *htsdyq* and *dikaioun* (neither of which admit a physical sense). Thus we magnify and justify God, not by making him great from small or just from unjust, but only declaratively celebrating him as such.

# A FALSE FOUNDATION

*Is the impulsive and meritorious cause (on account of which man is justified in the judgment of God) inherent righteousness infused into us or good works? We deny against the Romanists.*

Since it is evident from the preceding question that the word *justification* is forensic and is taken judicially here because it relates to the manner in which sinful man can stand before the bar of God and obtain the pardon of sin with a right to life, we must inquire before all things what is the foundation of this justification or what is the true and proper meritorious cause in view of which he is absolved by God from sin and adjudged to life. Concerning this we must first treat negatively (*kat' arsin*) according to the Pauline method in order that we may see in what it does not consist; second, we must treat affirmatively (*kata thesin*) to see in what it does consist.

However, we must premise here that God, the just Judge (*dikaiokritēn*), cannot pronounce anyone just and give him a right to life except on the ground of some perfect righteousness which has a necessary connection with life; but that righteousness is not of one kind. For as there are two covenants which God willed to make with men—the one legal and the other of grace—so also there is a twofold righteousness—legal and evangelical. Accordingly there is also a double justification or a double method of standing before God in judgment—legal and evangelical. The former consists in one's own obedience or a perfect conformity with the law, which is in him who is to be justified; the latter in another's obedience or a perfect observance of the law, which is rendered by a surety in the place of him who is to be justified—the former in us, the latter in Christ. Concerning the first, Paul says, "Not the hearers, but the doers of the law shall be justified" (Rom. 2:13); and "Moses describeth the righteousness which is of the law. That the man which doeth those things shall live by them" (Rom. 10:5). Concerning the other, he says, "The gospel is the power of God unto salvation to every one that believeth, for therein is the righteousness of God revealed from faith to faith: as it is written, The just shall live by faith" (Rom. 1:16–17); and "Being justified freely by his grace through the redemption that is in Christ Jesus" (Rom. 3:24). Concerning both, he says, "That I may be found in Christ, not having my own righteousness, which is of the law, but that which is through the faith of Christ" (Phil. 3:9; cf. also Rom. 9:30–31). Hence a twofold justification flows: one in the legal covenant by one's own righteousness according to the clause, "Do this and live"; the other in the covenant of grace, by another's righteousness (Christ's) imputed to us and apprehended by faith according to the clause, "Believe and thou shalt be saved." Each demands a perfect righteousness. The former requires it in the man to be justified, but the latter admits the vicarious righteousness of a surety. The former could have place in a state of innocence, if Adam had remained in innocence. But because after sin it became impossible to man, we must fly to the other (i.e., the gospel), which is founded upon the righteousness of Christ.

This being established, the question does not concern legal justification. For we confess that in it inherent righteousness is its meritorious cause, nor can it be obtained except by the perfect obedience of man. But because the law has now become weak by sin, this method of justification is impossible (*ek tōn adynatōn*). Thus we treat of the evangelical justification proposed to us in the covenant of grace, which we deny to be founded in inherent righteousness.

The question is not whether inherent righteousness is infused into us through the grace of Christ, by whose intervention we are made partakers of the divine nature (2 Peter 1:4) and obtain a true and real holiness pleasing and acceptable to God, by which we are properly denominated just and holy. For whatever the opponents may calumniously charge upon the orthodox (to wit, that "we allow of no inherent righteousness," as Bellarmine), it is surely a most foul calumny. Its falsity is proved from the writings of our divines whether public or private, in which everywhere and with common consent they teach that the benefits of justification and sanctification are so indissolubly connected with each other that God justifies no one without equally sanctifying him and giving inherent righteousness by the creating of a new man in true righteousness and holiness. But the question is whether that inherent righteousness (such as exists in believers on earth) enters into our justification, either as its cause or as a part, so that it constitutes some part of our justification and is the meritorious cause and foundation of our absolving sentence in the judgment of God. Romanists, as they pretend that justification consists of two parts—remission of sin and internal renovation of mind—so they assert that the cause on account of which God justifies us is the righteousness of God, which (infused into us)

11

constitutes us internally righteous. For although they do not appear to exclude entirely the righteousness of Christ, inasmuch as they hold that by it he merited that God should communicate to us by the Holy Spirit internal righteousness and thus it is a condition of the formal cause (i.e., of inherent righteousness that it may be given to man), still they maintain that the right to seek life depends upon inherent righteousness and that on account of it God justifies us.

This is evident from the Council of Trent where "the justification of the wicked is said to be the translation from that state in which man is born a son of the first Adam, into a state of grace and the adoption of the sons of God by the second Adam, Jesus Christ, our Savior. This translation indeed, after the promulgation of the gospel, cannot be made without the washing of regeneration or a desire for it." And: "Justification itself follows this disposition or preparation which is not only the remission of sin, but also sanctification and the renovation of the inward man by a voluntary reception of grace and gifts, by which a person who was unjust is made just and instead of an enemy becomes a friend, so that he is an heir according to the hope of eternal life." And afterwards: "The formal cause of it is the righteousness of God, not that by which he is himself righteous, but that by which he makes us righteous; and by which, bestowed upon us as his gift, we are renewed in the spirit of our mind and are not only accounted, but are truly called and are righteous, receiving each of us righteousness in ourselves, according to our measure, which the Spirit distributes to everyone as he wills and according to the peculiar disposition and cooperation of everyone." And Cannon 11: "If any man shall say that men are justified solely by the remission of sins to the exclusion of grace and charity which is shed abroad in our hearts by the Spirit and is inherent in them, or even that the grace by which we are justified is only the favor of God, let him be accursed." From these declarations, it is evident that the Council held that inherent righteousness is the cause on account of which we are justified. Nor ought we to be deceived by their seeming distinction between the formal and meritorious cause: the one indeed being Christ's, but the other infused righteousness. Since they speak of justification before God, the formal cause cannot be distinguished from the meritorious cause because in this respect the formal cause is nothing other than that in view of which God frees us from condemnation and receives us to eternal life.

On the other hand, the orthodox think far differently. For although they do not deny that inherent righteousness was purchased for us by the merit of Christ and by his grace conferred upon us so that by it we are and can be denominated truly just and holy, still they deny that it enters into justification in any way, either as a cause or as a part, so that justification may be said to be placed in it and by and on account of it man may be justified before God. For the righteousness of Christ alone imputed to us is the foundation and meritorious cause upon which our absolutary sentence rests, so that for no other reason does God bestow the pardon of sin and the right to life than on account of the most perfect righteousness of Christ imputed to us and apprehended by faith. Hence it is readily gathered that we have not here a mere dispute about words (as some falsely imagine), but a controversy most real and indeed of the highest moment. In it we treat of the principal foundation of our salvation, which being overthrown or weakened, all our confidence and consolation both in life and in death must necessarily perish.

This appears more clearly when we come to the thing itself and the controversy is not carried on coldly and unfeelingly in scholastic cloud and dust (as if from a distance), but in wrestling and agony—when the conscience is placed before God and terrified by a sense of sin and of the divine justice, it seeks a way to stand in the judgment and to flee from the wrath to come. It is indeed easy in the shades of the schools to prattle much concerning the worth of inherent righteousness and of works to the justification of men; but when we come into the sight of God, it is necessary to leave such trifles because there the matter is conducted seriously and no ludicrous disputes about words (*logomachia*) are indulged. Hither our eyes must be altogether raised if we wish to inquire profitably concerning true righteousness; in what way we may answer the heavenly Judge, when he shall have called us to account. Truly while among men the comparison holds good; each one supposes he has what is of some worth and value. But when we rise to the heavenly tribunal and place before our eyes that supreme Judge (not such as our intellects of their own accord imagine, but as he is described to us in Scripture [namely, by whose brightness the stars are darkened; at whose strength the mountains melt; by whose anger the earth is shaken; whose justice not even the angels are equal to bear; who does not make the guilty innocent; whose vengeance when once kindled penetrates even to the lowest depths of hell]), then in an instant the vain confidence of men perishes and falls and conscience is compelled (whatever it may have proudly boasted before men concerning its own righteousness) to deprecate the judgment and to confess that it has nothing upon which it can rely before God. And so it cries out with David, "Lord, if thou marked iniquity, who can stand?"; and elsewhere, "Enter not into judgment with thy servant, because no flesh will be justified in thy sight."

Here then is the true state of the controversy. When the mind is thoroughly terrified with the consciousness of sin and a sense of God's wrath, what is that thing on account of which he may be acquitted before God and be reckoned a righteous person? What is that righteousness which he ought to oppose to the judgment of God that he may not be condemned according to the strict demands of the law (*akribodikaion*), but may obtain remission of sins and a right to eternal life? Is it righteousness inhering in us and inchoate holiness or the righteousness and obedience of Christ alone imputed to us? Our opponents hold the former; we the latter. We are about to demonstrate this distinctly: (1) as to inherent righteousness; (2) as to imputed righteousness. Of the latter we will treat in the next question; of the former we speak now.

That inherent righteousness cannot be the meritorious cause of our justification, we prove: (1) because no one is justified by an imperfect righteousness, since the judgment of God is according to truth and in it there is no room for a gracious acceptation; nor can deception consist with his law and justice. But inherent righteousness is not perfect, nor actual, nor habitual. Not actual because in many things we all offend (James 3:2) and there is no one that sinneth not (1 Kings 8:46), which Bellarmine himself does not deny. Not habitual because the perfection and imperfection of an act depend upon the perfection or imperfection of the habit and our regeneration is always imperfect here (1 Cor. 13:12; Gal. 5:17). Nor ought it to be objected "that this absolute perfection was required under the law, but is not required under the gospel." The relaxation made under the gospel does not extend so far that an imperfect righteousness can be accepted for a perfect righteousness; for God cannot be satisfied except by a perfect righteousness. Rather it consists in this— that the vicarious and the alien righteousness of a surety is admitted for our own. Nor ought it to be objected "that righteousness is properly said to be perfect because it belongs to the works of God, which must be perfect because the work of the Rock is perfect" (Deut. 32:4). For the works which God does immediately by himself (which are rightly called perfect absolutely and simply) and the mediate works (which are performed by the intervention of creatures—such as the work of regeneration—which are not at once perfect because God operating according to our capacity promotes and perfects them little by little) differ.

Second, our justification takes place without works; therefore also without inherent righteousness, which consists wholly in works or in habits from which works spring. The passages are obvious. Scarcely anything has been said more often and asserted more constantly; nothing certainly more fully argued: "By the deeds of the law, there shall no flesh be justified" (Rom. 3:20); "We conclude, that a man is justified by faith without the deeds of the law" (v. 28). This the apostle confirms in Romans 4:6 and Galatians 2:16 and in many other places. Nor should it be replied here that all works are not absolutely excluded, but certain ones only (to wit, ceremonial); or if moral works are excluded, those only are meant which precede faith and grace and which are done by the strength of free will, not those which are done from faith and grace. Since the apostle absolutely and simply excludes all works without any exception, it does not become us to limit what he does not limit. The thing itself proves this also for he antithetically opposes faith to works in this matter. Hence it appears that all works entirely of whatsoever kind and not some particular ones are excluded. Otherwise he could not have simply opposed "one working" and "one believing," "to do" and "to believe," but a certain kind of working to other kinds.

This is demonstrated in particular (1) as to ceremonial works. For that law with its works is understood to be excluded by the apostle by which is the knowledge of sin (Rom. 3:20) and the whole world has become exposed to condemnation (v. 19). Concerning this it is said, "The man that doeth them shall live in them" (Gal. 3:12) and from the curse of which Christ redeemed us (v. 13). This must be understood of the whole law, especially the moral, not the ceremonial. (2) If the ceremonial law only would be excluded, not the moral (since it is the less principal part of the law), justification would have to be ascribed rather than denied to the law by reason of the moral law (which is much prior). (3) This objection is rejected by many Romanists—Lombard, Thomas Aquinas, Toletus, Pererius, Justiniani, Salmeron and others, as their commentaries clearly show. Lombard says, "Without any works of the law, even the moral." Thomas Aquinas says on this passage: "Without the works of the law, not only ceremonial, which do not bestow grace, but signify it, but also without the works of the moral precepts according to this, not by works of righteousness which we have done (Titus 3:5)." Nor if the controversy between Paul and the false apostles arose from the use of circumcision and the observance of the ceremonial law (which they urged as necessary to justification), does it follow that the apostle speaks of it alone when he excludes the works of the law from it. He passes from a part to the whole, this hypothesis of the false apostles drawing with it a necessity of observing the whole law (as we see in Acts 15:15) and Paul himself testifies when he says that he who presses circumcision as necessary "is a debtor to do the whole law" (Gal. 5:3) because the law demands not a partial, but a perfect obedience in all. Hence because he saw that believers would thus slide back to the old covenant and depart from the new, he inveighs with so much warmth against this error as most pestilential.

No better do others answer that it treats of works of the moral law done before faith and grace. (1) Paul excludes all works which are opposed to faith; yet all works without distinction are here opposed to faith, as working and believing are opposed (Rom. 4:5). (2) There was no necessity to exclude the works of the unregenerate, since it was acknowledged that they were sins, being done without faith (Rom. 14:23). (3) The examples of Abraham and David adduced by Paul (Rom. 4), inasmuch as they had been already converted and were believers, prove that works performed even after faith are excluded; as the apostle speaking of himself (now a believer) says, "I know nothing by myself; yet am I not hereby justified" (1 Cor. 4:4). (4) All those works are excluded which could leave any reason for boasting to man (Rom. 3:27). And yet such are works done by faith which they hold to be meritorious. (5) The works of believers are effects which follow justification, not the causes which precede it. (6) The design of the apostle in the epistle to the Galatians was to dispute against the false apostles who joined together in justification, faith and works, the grace of Christ and their own merits. (7) If he had wished to exclude only the works of nature and not the works of grace, why does he so often and so carefully oppose works to faith absolutely? Why does he never oppose the works of nature to the works of grace, which would have greatly assisted in refuting the calumny of his adversaries by which they assailed his doctrine, as if by excluding works from justification he would open the door to sin: "Shall we continue in sin, that grace may abound?" (Rom. 6:1). And yet that inference would be founded upon no foundation at all, if Paul had wished to exclude only works done before faith. For who otherwise would gather that sin must not be indulged in after faith on this account because works antecedent to faith do not justify in the least? Now both kinds of works being excluded, it was easy to object this very thing, which the Romanists of the present day object to us (to wit, that it is useless to do good works if there is no merit in works; nay, we should rather sin that grace may abound). This objection of the profane, the apostle did not refute by a distinction between antecedent and subsequent works (which assuredly he ought to have done according to the hypothesis of our opponents); but by an explanation of sanctification and its indissoluble connection with justification.

Third, "our justification is free by the grace of God, through the redemption of Christ" (Rom. 3:24). Here the grace of God cannot denote the infused habit of love (as Bellarmine holds), but the favor and benevolence of God because we are said to be justified by his grace (*tē autou chariti*) (i.e., as the leading [*proēgoumenē*] and meritorious cause is placed in the redemption of Christ, the false is rejected but the particle "freely" [*dōrean*], which excludes all merit in us). (2) This grace is opposed to works and boasting (Rom. 11:6, Eph. 2:9). (3) We cannot be justified by the redemption of Christ otherwise than by the imputation of his righteousness. This is incompatible (*asystatos*) with inherent righteousness in the matter of justification; for if we are justified in another, we cannot be justified in ourselves. (4) Pererius confesses that *charin* here denotes rather the gratuitous goodness and kindness of God towards men (which is elsewhere called "kindness" [*chrēstotēs*] and "love" [*philanthrōpia*] toward man, Titus 3:4). If the benevolence of God works good-pleasure (*eudokias*) in men (i.e., the good which he wills for them), it does not follow that he gives inherent righteousness that we may be justified by it. God does that good by distinct acts—the good indeed of imputed righteousness by the act of justification or inherent righteousness by the act of sanctification (as he has made Christ unto us both righteousness and sanctification, 1 Cor. 1:30).

Fourth, according to Paul justification consists in the remission of sins (Rom. 4:8). Nor can it be done otherwise, since a sinner is concerned. And yet he whose sin is freely pardoned cannot be justified by inherent righteousness; nor is inherent righteousness remission of sins. Nor does he escape who says that it is not indeed remission of sins, but still it is connected with it in justification. It involves a contradiction to say that man is justified at the same time by inherent righteousness and by remission of sins, as it is most absurd (*asystaton*) for one to be justified in himself and in another (by a personal and by another's obedience).

Fifth, if justification were by inherent righteousness, justification will be of the law, not of the gospel, and the two covenants will be confounded which are nevertheless constantly opposed as diametrically opposite to each other. Legal justification takes place in no other way than by inherent righteousness, whether actual or habitual; gospel justification is to be sought not in us, but in another. This the apostle clearly teaches when he wishes "to be found in Christ" (to wit, in the judgment of God) "not having his own righteousness, which is of the law, but that which is through the faith of Christ" (Phil. 3:9) (i.e., not an inherent righteousness, arising from an observance of the law and which is called ours because it is in us and is perfected by our actions, but the righteousness of God and Christ, imputed to us and apprehended by faith).

Sixth, this derogates from the merit of Christ and is an argument for glorying and pride. For if the righteousness and merit of Christ most fully suffice for our justification, why are human merits sewed on? Is not injury thus done to Christ and material given to man for glorying in himself with God? Nor is this absurdity removed by saying that all this righteousness depends on Christ, who obtained that also for us and gave to it the power of meriting. Besides the gratuitous assumption that Christ merited for us the power of meriting (as will be seen in the proper place), whatever good man receives from God by grace (according to their hypothesis) does not exclude the concourse of free will (by whose intervention man may have some material for glorying in himself, while we ought to glory in the Lord alone). The Pharisee is no less condemned, although giving thanks to God he professes that he has all that he has from him, not from himself (Luke 18:11–12, 14).

Seventh, remission of sin requires the removal of guilt by the payment of the ransom (*lytrou*) due. And yet inherent righteousness can neither remove the offense to God or the guilt springing from it, nor compensate for the injury to the divine majesty. For besides the fact that it looks to the future (that man may perform his duty), not to the past (that he may compensate for the defect of duty by giving a satisfaction), it is impossible by a quality of finite virtue and worth for an offense of infinite indignity to be blotted out and compensated for.

Eighth, we cannot omit here the remarkable testimonies of two cardinals, who, overcome by the power of the truth, agree with us. The first is Cardinal Contarini, who thus expresses himself: "Since we reach a twofold righteousness by faith, a righteousness inherent in us, and the love and grace by which we are made partakers of the divine nature; and the righteousness of Christ given and imputed to us, since we are planted in Christ and put on Christ: it remains to inquire, on which of these we ought to rest, and to think ourselves justified before God (i.e., reckoned holy and righteous). I truly think it to be said piously and religiously that we ought to rest, I say rest as upon a stable thing, which can certainly sustain us, upon the righteousness of Christ bestowed upon us, and not upon the holiness and grace inherent in us. For this our righteousness is inchoate and imperfect which cannot keep us from offending and from constantly sinning in many things. Therefore we cannot in the sight of God on account of this our righteousness be esteemed righteous and good, as it becomes the sons of God to be good and holy. But the righteousness of Christ given to us is a true and perfect righteousness. It is altogether pleasing in the sight of God. In it there is nothing that offends him; that does not in the highest degree please him. We must therefore rest upon this alone (sure and stable) and on account of it alone we must believe that we are justified before God, that is, considered righteous and called righteous." From him Bellarmine does not differ much, who, after exerting all his strength in a defense of human merit, pressed by the consciousness of the truth, at length is brought to say "that on account of the uncertainty of personal righteousness, and the danger of vain glory, it is the safest to place our entire confidence in the mercy and kindness of God alone." To this proposition answers this clause of his will: "And I pray him to admit me among his saints and elect, not as an estimator of merit, but as a bestower of pardon."

Christ by his obedience is rightly said "to constitute" us "righteous," not by an inherent but by an imputed righteousness as is taught in Romans 4:6 and gathered from the opposition of the antecedent condemnation (Rom. 5:19). For they are no less constituted righteous before God who, on account of the obedience of Christ imputed to them, are absolved from deserved punishment, than they who on account of the disobedience of Adam are constituted unrighteous (i.e., are exposed to death and condemnation). If Adam constituted us unrighteous effectively by a propagation of inherent depravity (on account of which we are also exposed to death in the sight of God), it does not follow equally that Christ constitutes us righteous by a forensic justification at the bar of God by inherent righteousness given to us by him. The design of the apostle (which alone is to be regarded) does not have this direction. He only wishes to disclose the foundation of the connection between being exposed to death and the right to life, from our union with the first and

second Adam, as to the thing (although the mode is different on account of the difference in the subject). The "abundance of grace and of righteousness" (*perisseia tēs charitos kai
dikaiosynēs*, Rom. 5:17) does not denote habitual grace or inherent righteousness, but the abundance of divine mercy
and the infinite treasury of righteousness, which believers
obtain in the obedience of the Mediator. And this gift is said
to be greater than the sin of Adam because the grace of God
giving us the righteousness of Christ, not only took away
the guilt of one transgression, but of all actual sins (as
Thomas Aquinas well remarks on this passage). Nor does it
press us more that we are said "to receive abundance of
grace" (Rom. 5:17) because we receive it by the hand of faith,
not that it becomes ours by way of infusion or of inhesion,
but by way of imputation.

"Justification" is not set forth as a genus, embracing under itself "ablution" and "sanctification" (1 Cor. 6:11), but on
the contrary "ablution," which is adumbrated in baptism; as
the more general word is set forth in the first place, contain-
ing under it justification and sanctification as two species,
as frequently both these benefits are wont to be described by
the one word—ablution, as much as justification (Ps. 51:2;
1 John 1:7) and as much as sanctification (Heb. 9:14). What
is added, however, concerning "the name of Christ" does
not properly denote an invocation, which is made by it, but
the power and efficacy of it—that "to be justified in the name
of Christ" is nothing else than to be justified by and on account of Christ. For there is no other name by which we can
obtain salvation.

Paul does not say that we are justified by regeneration (Titus 3:5–7); nay, since he ascribes justification to the grace of
God and takes it away from works, he shows that he is unwilling to ascribe it to righteousness inhering by regeneration, which is rather the fruit than the cause of justification.

But his intention is to point out how God will have us saved by two benefits which he bestows upon us—regeneration, of which the Holy Spirit is the author in us; and justification, which we obtain by Christ, by which we are made heirs of eternal life. That denotes the way of salvation, this its cause. The conformity to the image of Christ to which we are predestinated (Rom. 8:29) means indeed that we are made partakers of inherent holiness and righteousness like his; but it does not mean that we are justified by that inherent righteousness, as he was. For both our preceding sin and the imperfection of this righteousness in us renders such a justification impossible. For it cannot happen that they, who are the children of wrath by nature and who are never without sin, can be justified in the same manner in which he was justified, who knew no sin and in whose mouth no guile was found.

Although Abel and Noah were righteous and did good works, still they were not on that account justified by their own inherent righteousness and good works. Nay, Paul testifies that they were righteous by the righteousness of faith (Heb. 11): Abel in that by faith he offered a more excellent sacrifice, by which he also obtained witness that he was righteous (v. 4). Noah became heir of the righteousness which is by faith (v. 7), which is no other than the righteousness which God imputes through faith (Rom. 4:5–6). From this flowed the good works which they performed.

Since justification is described in the Scriptures by remission of sins and the imputation of righteousness, it cannot be called a motion from sin to righteousness, such as occurs in illumination and calefaction. And this is the fundamental error (*prōton pseudos*) of our opponents, who convert a forensic and judicial action (which takes place before God) into a physical or moral action (which takes place in us).

When believers seek to be justified by God according to their righteousness (Pss. 7:8; 17:1; 18:20), we must not understand it of a personal righteousness (of which they elsewhere confess they are destitute, Pss. 130:3; 143:2), but of a righteousness of the cause (which they maintained and on account of which they suffered persecution from the wicked); or if personal righteousness is understood by it, it is not universal and absolute (which is found in no mortal), but particular as to certain acts in which they can conduct themselves well by the grace of God (such as was the action of Phineas which was imputed to him for righteousness) and comparative, not relative to God, but to the wicked (who undeservedly slandered them).

The proportion of man to the highest good is either from the prescription of the law ("Do this and live") or from the assistance of grace. In the former sense, man in innocence would have had a proportion to the highest good. But by sin, that way having been shut up, another was to be sought in Christ, who by fulfilling the law for us, acquired for us a right to the highest good or eternal life. When therefore life is said to be given to the pious and righteous, the quality or disposition of the subject is denoted (which ought to possess life), not, however, the cause of such a good (i.e., how happy they ought to be, not why and on account of what).

Although in those to whom the satisfaction of Christ is imputed, the habit of righteousness is also infused (which we reach only in the other life and by this habit we begin to be righteous morally and inherently), still we cannot be called righteous relative to the divine judgment. For we are constituted righteous in the divine court only insofar as we can remove the accusation with which we are charged—of sin past as well as present. Now such an inchoate habit of righteousness cannot remove such an accusation, whether by making it false (because it is evident that we always have sinned and so are guilty) or by expunging it through a suffering of the punishment due (because it cannot have the relation of a satisfaction for sins committed by which their guilt may be taken away). For it tends to this—that we may not sin hereafter; but it cannot make us not to have sinned so that we do not need another's righteousness imputed to us for our justification.

# THE TRUE
# FOUNDATION

*Is the righteousness and obedience of Christ imputed to us the mer-
itorious cause and foundation of our justification with God? We
affirm against the Romanists and Socinians.*

The false and pretended impelling and meritorious cause
of our justification (which is placed by the Romanists in inherent righteousness) having been rejected, the true and genuine cause must now be exhibited from the Scriptures (to
wit, the righteousness and obedience of Christ imputed to
us by God). That the truth and mode of this may be the more
clearly seen and more strongly retained against the cavils of
our opponents, the following things must be premised.

First, we suppose that justification is a forensic act of God
(as has already been proved), not as a creditor and a private
person, but as a ruler and Judge giving sentence concerning
us at his bar. (2) Justification is the act not of a subordinate
Judge, who is bound to the formula of the law, but of a
supreme magistrate and prince, to whom alone belongs, in
virtue of his autocratic (*autokratorikō*) right, the showing of

favor to the guilty and the relaxation of the rigor of established laws. (3) That God does not here sit on the throne of justice that he may act according to the strict justice of the law (*kata to akribodikaion nomou*), but on the throne of grace that he may act according to the gospel forbearance (*epieikeian*). (4) That he so acts from mercy as not to do injury to his justice, which (since it cannot suffer his laws to be violated with impunity and sin to go unpunished) necessarily requires some satisfaction (*lytron*) to be made to it.

Hence it follows (5) that God cannot show favor to, nor justify anyone without a perfect righteousness. For since the judgment of God is according to truth, he cannot pronounce anyone just who is not really just. However, since no mortal after sin has such a righteousness in himself (nay, by sin he has been made a child of wrath and become exposed to death), it must be sought out of us in another, by the intervention of which man (sinful and wicked) may be justified without personal righteousness. Human courts often justify the guilty, either through ignorance (when the wickedness is not known and lies concealed) or by injury (when it is not attended to) or by iniquity (when it is approved). But in the divine court (in which we deal with the most just Judge, who neither holds the guilty as innocent, nor the innocent as guilty) this cannot occur. Therefore he who is destitute of personal righteousness ought to have another's, by which to be justified. For although God (as the supreme arbiter of affairs and the sovereign Lord of all) has the power to remit the punishment of sinners, still he cannot (because he is most just) thus favor the sinner, unless a satisfaction is first made by which both his justice may be satisfied and punishment taken of sin. Since this could not come from us who are guilty, it was to be sought in another, who (constituted a surety in our place by receiving upon himself the punishment due to us) might bestow the righteousness (*dikaiōma*) of which we were destitute.

The gospel teaches that what could not be found in us and was to be sought in another, could be found nowhere else than in Christ, the God-man (*theanthrōpō*); who taking upon himself the office of surety most fully satisfied the justice of God by his perfect obedience and thus brought to us an everlasting righteousness by which alone we can be justified before God; in order that covered and clothed with that garment as though it were of our first-born (like Jacob), we may obtain under it the eternal blessing of our heavenly Father.

Further, as long as Christ is outside of us and we are out of Christ, we can receive no fruit from another's righteousness. God willed to unite us to Christ by a twofold bond—one natural, the other mystical—in virtue of which both our evils might be transferred to Christ and the blessings of Christ pass over to us and become ours. The former is the communion of nature by the incarnation. By this, Christ, having assumed our flesh, became our brother and true Goel and could receive our sins upon himself and have the right to redeem us. The latter is the communion of grace by mediation. By this, having been made by God a surety for us and given to us for a head, he can communicate to us his righteousness and all his benefits. Hence it happens that as he was made of God sin for us by the imputation of our sins, so in turn we are made the righteousness of God in him by the imputation of his obedience (2 Cor. 5:21).

Just as Christ sustains a twofold relation (*schesin*) to us of surety and head (of surety, to take away the guilt of sin by a payment made for it; of head, to take away its power and corruption by the efficacy of the Spirit), so in a twofold way Christ imparts his blessings to us, by a forensic imputation, and a moral and internal infusion. The former flows from Christ as surety and is the foundation of our justification.

The latter depends upon him as head, and is the principle of sanctification. For on this account, God justifies us because the righteousness of our surety, Christ, is imputed to us. And on this account we are renewed because we derive the Spirit from our head, Christ, who renews us after the image of Christ and bestows upon us inherent righteousness.

However, because we treat here of the imputed righteousness of Christ, we must remark further that the word "impute" (which is in Hebrew *chshbh*; in Greek *logizesthai* or *ellogein*) can be taken in two ways, either properly or improperly. That is said to be imputed to anyone improperly which he himself has done or has, when on that account a reward or punishment is decreed to him. As sin is said "to be imputed" to the wicked (2 Sam. 19:19), when the reward of iniquity is imputed to them; and the judgment exercised by Phinehas "was counted unto him for righteousness" (Ps. 106:31), i.e., it was pleasing to God and gained for him the praise of holy zeal and the covenant of a perpetual priesthood. Properly is to hold him who has not done a thing, as if he had done it. In turn not to impute is to hold him who has done a thing as if he had not done it; as Paul desires the fault of Onesimus to be imputed to him (which he himself had not committed, Philem. 18) and asks that the fault should not be laid to the charge of those who forsook him (which they had committed, 2 Tim. 4:16). From this twofold acceptation of the word, a twofold imputation arises (about which Paul speaks)—of grace (*kata charin*) and of debt (*kat' opheilēma*): "Now to him that worketh is the reward not reckoned of grace, but of debt. But to him that justifieth the ungodly, his faith is counted for righteousness" (Rom. 4:4–5), viz., of grace. For the foundation of imputation is either in the merit and dignity of the person, to whom a thing is imputed; or it is out of it in the grace and mercy alone of the one imputing. The first is the legal mode, the other is the evangelical. Hence we gather that this word is forensic. It is not to be understood physically of an infusion of righteousness, but judicially and relatively, of gratuitous acceptance in the judgment of God (which also appears from the force of the word *logizesthai* and *ellogein*, which is drawn from accountants).

But here we must accurately distinguish between imputed and putative or fictitious in order to meet the calumny of our opponents who traduce this imputation as a mere fiction of the mind about a thing not existing. For it is a thing no less real in its own order (to wit, judicial and forensic) than infusion in a moral or physical order; as the imputation of a payment made by a surety to the debtor is in the highest degree real (to wit, by which he is freed from the debt and delivered from the right which the creditor had over him). Hence it is evident that this judicial act of God does not lack truth because he does not pronounce us righteous in ourselves (which would be false), but in Christ (which is perfectly true); nor does it lack justice because there is granted a communion between us and Christ, which is the solid foundation of this imputation.

Therefore when we say that the righteousness of Christ is imputed to us for justification and that we are just before God through imputed righteousness and not through any righteousness inherent in us, we mean nothing else than that the obedience of Christ rendered in our name to God the Father is so given to us by God that it is reckoned to be truly ours and that it is the sole and only righteousness on account of and by the merit of which we are absolved from the guilt of our sins and obtain a right to life; and that there is in us no righteousness or good works by which we can deserve such great benefits which can bear the severe examination of the divine court, if God willed to deal with us according to the rigor of his law; that we can oppose nothing to it except the merit and satisfaction of Christ, in which alone, terrified by the consciousness of sin, we can find a safe refuge against the divine wrath and peace for our souls.

Now although we hold that there is nothing in us which can be opposed at the bar of God for justification, still one would improperly conclude from this what our opponents falsely and slanderously charge upon us—that we recognize no inherent righteousness in believers and by reason of which they are truly reckoned righteous and holy with God. Thus that we teach that believers always remain wicked and unjust in themselves, and that the righteousness of Christ is imputed to us solely to cover our sins and not to take them away. Hence they take occasion to traduce our doctrine concerning the imputation of Christ's righteousness as impious and execrable. As we just now said, however, we hold these two benefits to be inseparable: that no one is justified by Christ who is not also sanctified and gifted with inherent righteousness (from which believers can truly be denominated holy and righteous although not perfectly in this life).

From these principles, the state of the question can be readily gathered. First, against the Socinians it is inquired, Are the righteousness, obedience and satisfaction of Christ imputed to us for righteousness? For as they deny the obedience and satisfaction of Christ were rendered for us, so they reject the imputation and application of that obedience and satisfaction and explode it as a human invention. The orthodox, however, think the obedience and satisfaction of Christ are imputed to us for righteousness inasmuch as they are reckoned ours by the gratuitous mercy of God and on account of them we are absolved from sin in God's court and pronounced just.

But against the Romanists, the question is not: (1) Is the righteousness of Christ the formal cause of our justification (i.e., is it the form by which man is constituted just inherently, as the Romanists understand it describing justification by the infusion of righteousness)? For since we have already proved that it is a forensic, not a physical act, the question regarding the internal formal cause is fruitless (which pertains to the blessing of sanctification). Rather the question concerns the meritorious and impulsive cause of the divine judgment or our absolving sentence. Not, Is the righteousness of Christ our formal and inherent righteousness subjectively? But, Is our righteousness real and sufficient imputatively, by which, if we are not formally righteous by inherent righteousness, still we are formally justified by the imputation of it, so that apart from it there is no other material of our righteousness before God?

(2) The question is not Is the Righteousness and merit of Christ imputed to us? For this the Romanists do not dare to deny. The Council of Trent says, "Christ by his most holy suffering on the cross merited justification for us, and satisfied God, the Father for us, and no one can be just, unless he to whom the merits of the suffering of our Lord Jesus Christ are communicated." Hence Vasquez says, "We grant there are imputed to us for a certain effect, not only those things that are in us, as sin, faith and righteousness, but also some things that are without us, as the merit and obedience of Christ, because not only the things that are in us, but also those without, in view of which something is given to us are said to be reckoned among our things for some effect, as if they were truly ours." Bellarmine also acknowledges this: "If the Protestants mean only this that the merits of Christ are imputed to us because they are given to us of God, and we can offer them to the Father for our sins, since Christ undertook the burden of satisfying for us and reconciling us to God, the Father, their opinion is correct." And yet we mean nothing else; for what he adds ("that we wish the righteousness of Christ to be so imputed to us that by it we are called, and are formally righteous"), he supposes falsely and

gratuitously from his perverse and preposterous hypothesis concerning moral justification. But the question is To what is that imputation made? To justification and life, as we maintain; or only to the infusion of internal grace and inherent righteousness, as they hold? That is, are the merits of Christ so imputed and communicated to us as to be the sole meritorious cause of our justification and that there is no other righteousness on account of which we are acquitted in the sight of God (which we contend for); or are they so imputed as to be the conditions of a formal cause that is of inherent righteousness, so that man can be gifted with it; or of an extrinsic cause which deserves the infusion of righteousness by which man is justified, so that not the merit of Christ properly, but inherent righteousness acquired by the merit of Christ is the proper and true cause on account of which man is justified (which they maintain)? They so limit the benefit of the imputation of Christ's merits to obtaining the effect of infused grace that this imputation is made for no other end than to merit for us infused grace, in virtue of which we obey the law and, being righteous in ourselves, are justified; as Vasquez, in the passage cited, observes. Hence Bonaventure denies that the causality of justification or of the remission of sins properly belongs to the death or resurrection of Christ, but only "by way of intervening merit," which is reduced to the material cause, while he determines the formal cause to be infused love. From these it is evident that the question here is Are the righteousness and satisfaction of Christ so imputed to us by God as to be the only foundation and meritorious cause in view of which alone we are acquitted before God of our sins and obtain a right to life? Our opponents deny; we affirm.

However, there is no need to remark that by the righteousness of Christ we do not understand here the "essential righteousness of God" dwelling in us (as Osiander with

Schwenkfeld dreamed, opposing himself to Stancar his colleague, who acknowledged Christ as Mediator only according to his human nature—which error was exploded and perished with its author). That righteousness could not be communicated to us subjectively and formally which is an essential attribute of God without our becoming gods also. And the Scripture everywhere refers the righteousness of Christ, which is imputed to us, to the obedience of his life and the suffering of his death, by which he answered the demands of the law and perfectly fulfilled it. If we had need of an infinite righteousness, it should not be such in essence, but only in value and merit. If Christ is Jehovah, our righteousness, and if he is made to us righteousness by the Father, this is not said with respect to essential righteousness, but to the obedience which is imputed to us for righteousness. This is called the righteousness of God because it belongs to a divine person and so is of infinite value and is highly pleasing and acceptable to God. By this righteousness then, we understand the entire obedience of Christ—of his life as well as of his death, active as well as passive.

Now that this righteousness of Christ is the foundation and meritorious cause of our justification, we prove: (1) because by the righteousness and obedience of one, Christ, we are constituted righteous—"As by the offense of one" (supply "guilt") "came upon all men to condemnation, even so by the righteousness of one" (*di' henos dikaiōmatos*) (supply "the blessing redounded") "upon all men unto justification of life. For as by one man's disobedience many were made sinners, so by the obedience of one shall many be made righteous" (Rom. 5:18–19). Here it is clear that the one transgression (*hen paraptōma*) is opposed to the one righteousness (*heni dikaiōmati*) and the disobedience of one man (by which men are constituted sinners and guilty before God by the imputation of that sin) is opposed to the obedience of one,

35

Christ, by which the elect are constituted righteous (i.e., are justified before God; not assuredly by inhesion, but by imputation). (a) The act of one cannot be made the act of many, except by imputation. (b) The righteousness (*dikaiōma*) upon which justification of life (*dikaiōsis zōēs*) rests, demands a perfect and absolute righteousness (which cannot be said of inherent righteousness). (c) The condemnation (*katakrima*) to which the justification of life (*dikaiōsis zōēs*) is opposed, is not a physical, but a forensic and judicial act. In vain does Bellarmine maintain that the obedience of Christ is indeed the efficient but not the formal cause of justification, as the disobedience of Adam constituted us sinners, not formally but efficiently. We are not treating of an infusion of righteousness or of renovation (as we have just said), but of a juridical constitution which cannot take place except by imputation (since it is of another's, not of a personal righteousness). Again, Bellarmine himself testifies the contrary when he says, "The sin of Adam is so imputed to his posterity, as if we had all committed the same sin." And: "The sin of Adam is communicated to us in the manner in which what passes over can be communicated, to wit, by imputation; for it is imputed to all who are born of Adam." Nor if we are constituted unrighteous and guilty by sin propagated from Adam, ought we at once to be justified by inherent righteousness communicated to us through regeneration by Christ because there is a very different reason for each. And Paul here institutes the comparison between the first and second Adam in the thing and not as to the manner of the thing.

 Second, faith is said to be imputed to us for righteousness. "Abraham believed God, and it was counted unto him for righteousness" (Rom. 4:3); not the faith itself or the act of believing formally, as if it were righteousness with God (as the Remonstrants hold, against whom we will dispute hereafter)

because thus justification would not be without works, since faith itself is a work; but objectively and relative to the righteousness of Christ, which faith apprehends and applies to itself. The apostle calls this "the righteousness of faith which is through the faith of Christ" (Phil. 3:9) "in which alone he wishes to be found" (viz., at the bar of God). For it is to be sought nowhere else than in Christ, who is Jehovah our righteousness, and who of God is made unto us righteousness. It is confirmed by this—that Paul in the same place explains the imputation of faith for righteousness by "the imputation of righteousness without works" (Rom. 4:6). Hence it is surely evident: (a) that justification consists in the imputation of righteousness, that no one may suppose this phrase was invented by us; (b) that this righteousness cannot be inherent, given to us by infusion, both because it is said to be without works and because what is inherent is opposed to what is imputed. On that account, it is opposed by Paul to his own righteousness which is of the law (Phil. 3:9) and is elsewhere called "the righteousness of God," which is manifested without the law (Rom. 3:21–22). This is so because it is subjectively in a divine person and so of infinite value; and originally because it is from God, since it is given to us freely by God; and terminatively because it leads to God and is approved by him and can alone sustain the examination of his judgment. Therefore whoever by faith applies that righteousness to himself is said not to come into judgment, but to have already passed from death to life (John 5:24), i.e., to be justified.

Third, Christ is the righteousness by which we are justified. For on this account he is said to "be made of God unto us righteousness" (1 Cor. 1:30) and we are said to be made the righteousness of God in him: "God hath made him to be sin for us, who knew no sin; that we might be made the righteousness of God in him" (2 Cor. 5:21). From this it is evident: (a) that Christ is our righteousness before God, not surely inherently (because the righteousness of one cannot pass over into another), but imputatively; (b) we are made the righteousness of God in him, just as he is made sin for us. Now Christ was made sin for us, not inherently or subjectively (because he knew no sin), but imputatively (because God imputed to him our sins and made the iniquities of us all to meet on him, Isa. 53:6). Therefore, we also are made righteousness, not by infusion, but by imputation. Augustine well expresses this: "He, therefore, was sin, that we might be righteousness, nor ours, but God's, nor in us, but in him, as he demonstrated sin, not his own, but ours, nor in himself, but in us constituted in the likeness of sinful flesh, in which he was crucified." The objection is fruitless that "Christ is said to have been made righteousness, as he was made wisdom and sanctification, not surely imputatively, but effectively." For even if he was equally made to us of God all these as to merit because he acquired all these blessings for us, still he was not made in the same manner as to bestowal, but diversely according to the diversity of the gifts (even the nature of the thing demands this). For if he was made righteousness in no other way than sanctification (i.e., effectively), Paul would be guilty of tautology, since in this way justification and sanctification would not differ. Therefore he is made wisdom and sanctification to us effectively by illuminating and regenerating us; but righteousness imputatively by imputing to us his righteousness. Bellarmine cannot deny this when he says that Christ can rightly be said to be made righteousness meritoriously "because he satisfied the Father for us, and gives and communicates that satisfaction to us, when he justifies us, so that he can be called our satisfaction and righteousness, as if we ourselves had satisfied God." This he confirms on 2 Corinthians 5:21: "The righteousness of Christ is imputed to us as to the satisfaction, which he made for us." Nor can that which our opponent adds in the same place help his cause when he says: "But not on this account can we be reckoned righteous, if the stains and corruption of sins truly inhere in us." For if the righteousness of Christ is imputed to us (as he had already confessed), then certainly we are considered righteous in him; for no one imputes righteousness to him whom he does not count righteous. And if the satisfaction of Christ is imputed to us, then our debts for which he satisfied are not imputed, but are remitted. Falsely also he holds "that the righteousness inhering in us is here called the righteousness of God because it is given to us of God; or also because it is the image and effect of the righteousness of God." For the little clause "in him" stands in the way; for how could it be said to be in Christ, if it was in us? Contarini acknowledges this: "The righteousness of God in him, since his righteousness is made ours, is given and imputed to us."

Fourth, justification takes place on account of the surety-ship of Christ and the payment made for us by him—which cannot be done without imputation. For as a payment made by a surety for a debtor cannot help him except by imputation (inasmuch as the payment made by a surety is applied to him as if it had been made by himself), the cancelling of the debt follows and the deliverance of the debtors. Thus since Christ undertook to be our surety and paid in our place, who does not see that the payment made by him and the ransom (*lytron*) given is imputed to us for full absolution (i.e., is considered by God as if it had been given by us)? In this sense, we are said to be "justified by the death and blood of Christ" (Rom. 5:9) because the merit of his obedience and death was that in view of which God was reconciled and gave to us the pardon of sin. In the same sense, he is said "to have been made a curse and sin for us, that we might be made a blessing and righteousness in him" (Gal. 3:13; 2 Cor.

5:21) because the curse and punishment of sin which he received upon himself in our stead secures to us blessing and righteousness with God in virtue of that most strict union between us and him by which, as our sins are imputed to him, so in turn his obedience and righteousness are imputed to us. Just as under the law the punishment which the victims suffered in the place of sinners was imputed to them for the expiation of sin and their liberation.

 Fifth, Christ justifies us by that by which he frees us from the condemnation of the law and fulfills in us its right to life. "For what the law could not do, in that it was weak through the flesh, God sending his own Son in the likeness of sinful flesh, and for sin, condemned sin in the flesh: that the righteousness of the law might be fulfilled in us" (namely, our justification by the law having become impossible through sin, God restored this benefit to us in Christ). Being made like to sinful flesh (yet without sin), he offered himself for us as a victim for sin and having made a most full satisfaction condemned sin (i.e., perfectly expiated it) in the flesh for this end—that the condemnation of sin might give place to our justification and the righteousness of the law (*to dikaiōma nomou*) (i.e., the right which it has) whether as to obedience or as to punishment is fulfilled in us (not inherently, but imputatively); while what Christ did and suffered in our place is ascribed to us as if we had done that very thing. Thus we are considered in Christ to have fulfilled the whole righteousness of the law because in our name he most perfectly fulfilled the righteousness of the law as to obedience as well as to punishment.

Sixth, our justification is "a justification of the ungodly but to him that worketh not, but believeth on him that justifieth the ungodly, his faith is counted for righteousness" (Rom. 4:5). A justification of the ungodly cannot be made by infusion, but by imputation. For although he that is justified does not remain wicked, but is renewed by the grace of Christ, he cannot be said to be justified by that renovation (which is the effect following justification, not the cause which precedes it). And faith, by which man is justified and is made righteous in Christ, does not prevent him from being and being called wicked in himself, inasmuch as he is opposed to the one working as he who has nothing upon which he can rely before the divine tribunal for his justification and so is "ungodly," partly antecedently, partly with respect to justification; not however concomitantly, still less consequently.

Various testimonies of the fathers could be gathered together here. By their vote, they approve our opinion, but we omit them from a desire to be brief. It will be sufficient to quote the words of Bernard because he often asserted this saving doctrine with exceeding skill: "Another's righteousness is assigned to him who wanted a personal righteousness." And a little after: "If one died for all, therefore all are dead; that the satisfaction of one might be imputed to all, as that one bore the sins of all." And: "My merit then is the compassion of the Lord; I am not wholly destitute of merit, as long as he is not wanting in mercy." And a little after: "Shall I sing of my righteousness? O Lord, I will make mention of thy righteousness alone, which is also mine. Shall I fear that one righteousness is not enough for both? It is not a short garment which according to the prophet cannot cover two." And: "Not to sin is the righteousness of God; the righteousness of man is the indulgence of God."

Christ ought not only to restore the goods lost in Adam, but also to remove the evils contracted through Adam. Now there were two—guilt and corruption of nature—to which two goods should be opposed: the imputation of righteousness to take away guilt before God; and a renovation of nature to heal inherent corruption. Again, Christ not only restored the lost goods, but in a far more excellent way. We lost mutable righteousness, but an immutable righteousness is restored to us. We lost only an inherent righteousness and there is given us an imputed righteousness with an inherent, without which we could not be made partakers of the inherent. Otherwise if nothing was restored in Christ than what had been lost in Adam, pardon of sin would not be given to us in Christ because it was not lost in Adam.

What is imputed to anyone by a mere gracious acceptation, that is not really paid, but is considered as paid; but what is imputed on account of a true payment made by another supposes the thing to be paid. Now the imputation of the righteousness of Christ (of which we speak) is not to be understood in the first sense (the improper sense, for an imputation which takes place without any payment at all whether of the debtor or of the surety); but is to be understood in the latter sense inasmuch as it is founded in another's payment (that of Christ the surety).

Although we are justified by the imputed righteousness of Christ, it does not follow that we are no less righteous than Christ and are thus considered like Christ, saviors and redeemers of the world; and that Christ on account of our unrighteousness imputed to him can be called a sinner. The dignity of the head ought always to remain his own, that the members may be conformed to the head; but in their order and not that they should become the head. Thus although as to imputation we are truly righteous in the sight of God, still Christ is righteous in a far more perfect manner. We are such relatively in him and indeed precariously and dependently; Christ, however, is such infinitely, originally, inherently and subjectively. (2) Indeed we can (on account of Christ's righteousness imputed to us) be said to be redeemed and saved passively, but not to be redeemers actively because he alone can be a Redeemer whose righteousness is imputed to another; not he who needs the imputation of another. (3) Christ cannot (on account of our sin having been imputed to him) be called a sinner (which implies inherent corruption), but only a victim for sin, who received on himself the punishment due to sin. Thus guilt was to be taken away, not its pollution.

Where two contrary physical forms and qualities exist under the same genus, there it is certain that the denomination should be made from the intrinsic (which affect the subject more), than from the extrinsic. Now inherent righteousness and imputed righteousness are not under the same genus. The former indeed is in the class of relation, but the latter is under the class of quality. Thus nothing is to hinder the subject from being denominated from both under a different respect (*schesei*). For when the inherent quality is regarded, he is said to be a sinner and wicked; but when the external and forensic relation is considered, he is said to be righteous in Christ. It is indeed true that no one can be called righteous inherently by another's righteousness because if it is inherent, it is no longer another's. But still he can be said to be justified imputatively, since every day among men a debtor (on account of the payment made by a surety) is said to be free and discharged. Augustine beautifully explains this: "It is surely just, that they whom the devil held as debtors, should be discharged believing in him whom he killed without any debt." Hence it is evident that the example of the Ethiopian adduced by Bellarmine (who is to be denominated rather from the blackness of his body than from the whiteness of his garments) is improper (*aprosdionyson*) since we are not speaking here of an inherent quality or of an adhering garment, but of a juridical relation given to him by the Judge. Besides, the Ethiopian always remains an Ethiopian in the same manner; yet the believer does not remain wicked, but is converted.

Although God justifies us on account of the imputed righteousness of Christ, his judgment does not cease to be according to truth because he does not pronounce us righteous in ourselves subjectively (which would be false), but in another imputatively and relatively (which is perfectly true). Thus God truly estimates the thing and judges it as it is; not in itself and in its own nature, but in Christ.

The spouse is said to be "all fair" (Cant. 4:7) in two ways (1) in her head and husband imputatively, when all her pollutions are so covered by his righteousness that there is no more condemnation in her; nor does God see in her anything as to practical and penal knowledge which he can reprehend; (2) in herself inherently because she has been perfectly renewed by the Spirit, if not with a perfection of degrees, still with a perfection of parts and of grace which will at length be crowned by a perfection of glory.

Although the imputed righteousness of Christ is maintained by us to be the foundation of our justification before God, it does not on that account cease to be purely gratuitous on our part. It is a mere gift of God's mercy because the sponsor is given to us of God and was substituted in our place and because his obedience and righteousness (which we ourselves ought to have rendered from the rigor of the law) is reckoned ours and imputed to us by God. And what is more, the righteousness of the law is fulfilled in us (Rom. 8:4) and justification thus ceases to be of the works of the law performed by us, that still it is not made against it, but in accordance with it and the law is not only made void but is rather established by faith (Rom. 3:31).

Although justification can be called extrinsic objectively (inasmuch as it is the imputation of righteousness which is formally without us), still it is ours terminatively. Nor is it more absurd for the righteousness of Christ to be extrinsic to us and yet to be imputed to us than it is absurd for our sins to be extrinsic to Christ and yet to be imputed to Christ for punishment; or (*ad hominem*) than it is absurd for the satisfaction of saints to be imputed to others, as the Romanists maintain.

As the disobedience of Adam truly constituted us sinners by imputation, so also the righteousness of Christ truly justifies us by imputation. Thus "imputed" is properly opposed to "inherent," but not to "true" because we do not invent an imputation consisting in a mere opinion and fiction of law; but one which is in the highest sense real and true. Yet this truth belongs to imputation, not to infusion; is juridical, not moral.

The righteousness of Christ is rightly said to be imputed to us for righteousness, not that it may be reckoned righteousness (which was already so before), but that what was before another's may be made ours and that on account of it we may be pronounced righteous and received to eternal life.

# 4

# JUSTIFICATION AND ADOPTION

*Does justification consist only in the remission of sins? Or does it embrace also adoption and the right to life? The former we deny and affirm the latter.*

We have discussed the meritorious cause or the foundation of justification. We must now treat of its form or parts. In this matter, the opinions of theologians vary.

Some contend that the whole of justification is comprehended in the remission of sin alone, so that God is to be considered as justifying us when he pardons our sins and absolves us from all punishment. They also hold this opinion who maintain that Christ's passive righteousness alone is imputed to us. However, others make justification to consist of two parts: remission of sin and imputation of righteousness. The former removes punishment from the sinner; the latter renders him worthy of the reward or of life.

But neither opinion seems to us to explain this subject with sufficient accuracy. Not the first because (as we shall afterwards say) absolution from punishment is not sufficient for a full justification, but the communication of a right to life is also required. If the orthodox sometimes assert that justification is contained in the remission of sins alone, it does not follow that they do not also acknowledge the right to life under it. For they speak thus against the Romanists, who hold that to justification pertains not only the remission of sins, but also an internal renovation of the soul and an infusion of righteousness. Against these they well maintain that the whole of justification consists in the remission of sins, under which they embrace also the right to life, exclusive of the renovation of man or the infusion of righteousness.

But neither can the second opinion be received simply because in it are falsely joined the remission of sins and the imputation of righteousness, as if they were parts answering to each other: remission indeed the first; imputation of righteousness another. However they do not in turn correspond with each other as a part to a part, but as a cause to an effect and a foundation to that which rests upon it and depends upon it. For if we wish to philosophize correctly, God does not remit our sins and afterwards impute righteousness, but he first imputes righteousness and afterwards on account of that imputed righteousness, remits our sins. For a satisfaction and a ransom (*lytron*) must necessarily intervene in order that remission may be granted by God without detriment to his justice and that it may be the foundation of the absolving sentence which is made in favor of the elect. If by the imputation of righteousness, theologians mean nothing else than the bestowal of a right to life (as it is certain many do), they hold that indeed truly, but do not express themselves with sufficient accuracy.

Thus then we believe the thing may be more readily and clearly conceived. Christ having been destined and given of God to us as a surety and head, in virtue of this union it happens that whatever was done by him (or endured for the perfect fulfillment of the law as to its precepts as well as to its penal sanction) is reckoned ours, as done in our place, and is imputed to us by God as if it had been performed by ourselves. From this imputation of his most perfect righteousness flow two benefits—both remission of sins and the bestowal of a right to life or adoption (in which two the whole of justification is contained). Thus the imputation of righteousness is the foundation and the meritorious cause of justification, while adoption and absolution are two parts of justification and effects of the imputation of righteousness which are inseparable from each other. For as pardon of sin cannot be granted nor a right to life be conferred, except on the supposition of the imputation of righteousness (by the intervention of which God can without prejudice to his justice free from punishment and bestow life), so, such imputation being posited, both these benefits flow necessarily from the double property of this righteousness, inasmuch as it has a satisfactory and meritorious power at the same time. By reason of the former, imputed righteousness is the foundation of the remission of sins; by reason of the latter, it is the cause of the right to life.

Now many reasons prove that these two benefits must be joined together here, whether we attend to the law (which was to be fulfilled) or regard our necessity, or the nature of things, or the voice of Scripture. For as the law contains a sanction of two parts—on the one side the punishment of death to transgressors; on the other, the reward of life to the obedient—so the righteousness of the law (which by the justification of Christ is fulfilled in us) cannot be obtained except with the remission of sins (which involves a liberation from punishment). We have a right to life which Christ acquired for us most perfectly by his obedience.

Second, the necessity of salvation demanded this very thing. Two evils were conveyed to us by sin: (1) that we were made guilty before God; (2) that we were made enemies and aliens from God, the fountain of life—the guilt of death into which we enter and the privation of life which we lost. And thus we could not be restored to integrity unless the guilt of death were taken away by the remission of sins and a right to life were given by adoption. As happiness is placed not only in a privation of evil, but most especially in the possession of good, it was not enough to be delivered from evil or death, unless also the right to good or life had been conferred.

Third, the nature of the thing proves it. It is one thing to redeem from punishment; another to assign a reward also. It is one thing to deliver from death; another to bestow life and happiness. It is one thing to bring out of prison; another to seat upon a throne. The former takes away evil, but the latter superadds good also; as if a fugitive slave should not only be acquitted of the punishment due, but also raised to the dignity and right of a son. For although these two things are connected together indissolubly from the covenant of grace, still from the nature of the thing they could be separated; as Adam, although innocent from the beginning of his creation and worthy of no punishment, still was not at once worthy of a reward until he had perfected the round of obedience, so it was not absolutely necessary that he whose sins have been remitted and who is delivered from the guilt of death, should straightway be gifted with a crown of immortality (since, if it pleased God, he might have afterwards directed man to work by which he should obtain the reward). Liberty certainly necessarily follows deliverance from prison, but not immediately the crown and throne. Joseph freed from his chains ought not on that account to be set over Egypt. Mephibosheth, brought out from squalor and thirst, was not immediately to be carried to the king's table. Thus two things must be distinctly conceived of in this benefit: the pardon of sin committed with a deliverance from the curse of the law; and a bestowal of the reward or blessing.

In many places, Scripture connects and distinguishes these. "Christ was made under the law [*hypo nomon*] to redeem them that were under the law" (Gal. 4:4–5) (to wit, as to the curse that we might receive the adoption of sons; i.e., the right to life which flows from adoption). Paul elsewhere confirms this: "by which faith we receive forgiveness of sins, and inheritance (*klēron*) among them which are sanctified" (Acts 26:18) (i.e., a right to eternal life with other saints). Here belongs the gradation between peace and glory which he weaves together when he says that "being justified we have peace with God, and rejoice in hope of the glory of God" (Rom. 5:1–2). Peace has reference to deliverance from punishment and glorying supposes the bestowal of a right to life, which is the foundation of our hope. On this account, he joins together "the being saved from wrath" and "glorying in God" (Rom. 5:9, 11). This very thing Daniel had already intimated when he ascribes to the Messiah, who was about to come, "a propitiation of iniquity" (by whom remission would be obtained) and "the bringing of an everlasting righteousness" (by whose power a right to life would be given, Dan. 9:24). Nor does Christ mean anything else when he promises believers "a transition from death to life" (i.e., not only deliverance from death, but also the possession of life). John means the same thing when he says that Christ not only "washes us from sin" by obtaining their pardon, but also "makes us kings and priests" who obtain the right to happiness and glory (Rev. 1:5–6).

Hence it appears that they are deceived who hold that the remission of sins and the imputation of righteousness differ only by reason of the diverse terms from which (*a quo*), and to which (*ad quem*); as it is not the covering of nakedness and the putting on of a garment, for this reason that sin and righteousness are contraries (*ameta*), one of which being posited the other is taken away. For it is far otherwise with these things, as we have already said. They are so to be joined together, as still not to be confounded, but to be distinguished as really differing from each other; or if the imputation of righteousness is put for a right to life, it is with respect to remission after the manner of part, constituting with it the form of justification. Hence they are not to be compared with each other as the covering of nakedness and the putting on of a garment (which are really one and the same thing), but as deliverance from punishment and royal dignity in a guilty person.

Sin and righteousness are indeed direct contraries (*ameta*), but not the righteousness which signifies perseverance in righteousness and perfection itself. For it is one thing to be free from corruption, but another to have persisted in duty and to have acquired merit. Adam had the former, not the latter. Thus between death and life there is no middle ground; but between eternal death and a happy life the middle ground is the mortal and animal life, a pious and holy life—but on earth, not in heaven, under the obligation of meriting by obedience. So many things could still come in between the flames of hell and the joys of heaven, deliverance from punishment and the possession of the reward; the punishment of slaves and the dignity of sons. Who, therefore, confers upon us (who were slaves adjudged to eternal punishment) adoption and an inheritance, will he not also wonderfully increase the benefit? It was much for us to be manumitted and to be made freedmen; now to be pronounced children and heirs, this is the climax and crowning blessing of mercy.

When Paul argues from the remission of sins to the imputation of righteousness (Rom. 4:5–7), he does not do this on account of their equivalency, as if these two do not differ from each other and signify one and the same thing. Rather he does it on account of the undivided connection between both because remission of sins can be given to no one, except on account of the imputation of righteousness and imputation of righteousness is given to no one without his sins being forthwith pardoned.

Although he who obtains the remission of all his sins (of omission as well as of commission) is freed from punishment (which he deserved on account of those sins) and thus far can be pronounced righteous (or rather justified and acquitted), still, accurately speaking, he cannot on that account be considered to have omitted nothing really good and to have committed nothing evil. God by remission reckons a man not unrighteous, not because he judges him never to have sinned and to be without a stain, but because he forgives and pardons the guilty whatever evil he has committed. However to pardon and, on account of recitude of conduct (*katorthōmata*), to reckon worthy of a reward and to honor, are far different.

# 5

# THE REMISSION
# OF SINS

*Does remission of sins consist in an absolute removal of them? Or in the pardon of them? And after the guilt is remitted is a certain punishment retained? Or is it wholly remitted? The former we deny; the latter we affirm against the Romanists.*

Because various questions are wont to be agitated concerning the remission of sins, we much touch briefly upon them under three propositions.

The first: remission of sins does not consist in a removal of the corruption or depraved quality, but in a gratuitous pardon of the criminality and guilt arising from it. This is opposed to the Romanists, who, to support their hypothesis concerning physical justification by infusion, maintain that remission of sin consists in a real taking away of it, as to corruption as well as to guilt. Thus an infusion of righteousness always succeeds remission, as light always follows the scattering of the clouds of darkness.

But the following arguments prove the falsehood of this opinion. (1) The mode of speaking and the proper signification of remission among men, which does not imply the extinction of sin, but only the pardoning of it (as a prince, by remitting a crime, does not take it away, but only pardons it and frees it from the punishment due on account of it). (2) The synonymous phrases of Scripture teach the same thing when remission is expressed by a "covering" (Ps. 32:1). Not that they are not, but that in the sight of God the Judge, they do not come into condemnation. For this reason, we ought to put on Christ that his righteousness may cover our sins before God. By a "not imputing" (Ps. 31:2) that on account of them we may not be punished as we deserve. By a "not remembering" (Jer. 31:34) that God may not deal with them practically according to his justice in punishing them. By a "blotting out" (Pss. 51:1; 103:12; Acts 3:19; Col. 2:14) not of the corruption but of the guilt, as a creditor expunges from his account book a debt from which he wishes to release the debtor by destroying and blotting out the very handwriting that it may no longer have any force. Even so God destroys the sins which are written in his book and for which we are accountable (*hypodikoi*) when he pardons them by freeing us from the guilt which attached to us on account of them. By a "casting of them behind his back" and "throwing them into the sea" (Mic. 7:19) that they may no more come into judgment. By a "purging" by way of propitiation and of offering (*hilasmou*, Heb. 1:3; 9:14) that the guilt of sin (which makes us hateful and abominable to God) may be cleansed; in allusion to the sprinkling (*rhantismon*) of the old sacrifices, which did not take away inherent pollution, but adhering guilt. By a "turning away" of "his face" (Ps. 51:9) and a "putting away" (2 Sam. 12:13) and similar phrases which rightly mean a juridical pardoning of guilt, not a real removal of pollution.

(3) If remission of sin was the taking away of inherent corruption, as the former is perfect, so also the latter ought to

be perfect (which is repugnant to Scripture, which testifies that sin always remains in us and belongs to the experience of saints, who always complain of the struggles of the flesh and the Spirit). (4) If not to impute sin is to expel it and to infuse righteousness; from the opposite, to impute sin will be to infuse sin. The falsity of this appears from the case of Christ, to whom sin was imputed, but not infused.

Although by remission of sins actual guilt or the obligation to punishment is taken away, potential guilt is not immediately taken away or the intrinsic merit of sin (which flows from its inherent corruption) because remission consists only in this—that the guilty person is freed by the Judge from the actual punishment due to him, not however immediately from all vitiosity. Hence Paul indeed says there is no condemnation to them which are in Christ (Rom. 8:1), but he does not say there is nothing condemnable or worthy of condemnation. For as long as sin remains in us (now it remains as long as we live), there is always something condemnable, although on account of the interceding grace of the Judge it does not any more actually condemn us.

There is a theoretical covering of sinners which belongs to omniscience, according to which it is certain that nothing can be covered by God except what he wholly destroys and abolishes; another practical (which has respect to the exercise of justice and thus can be covered by him)—what is still in the subject, when God does not see it so as to notice it, is blotted out of his book so that it may not come into account. Thus sins are said to be covered before God not because they are absolutely taken away (as they are not), but because they are not allotted to punishment. Hence Augustine says, "Therefore, why does he say his sins are covered? In order that they might not be seen. For what was it for God to see sins except to punish them?"

Although the remission of sins is expressed by various phrases (which denote a real taking away), it does not follow that they imply a total abolition of sin because in remission there is something real, since by it the actual obligation to punishment and the punishment itself are really and truly taken away from the person. Again, these phrases (such as "to take away," "to bear away," "to remove," "to wash out," "to purge sins") are partly explained by others which signify the removal of guilt (not however the nonexistence of sin) and are partly drawn from the effect of sacrifices, which was the propitiation and purgation of sin; not by a removal of its corruption, but by a taking away of the guilt and a giving away (*condonationem*) of the punishment.

Although we do not deny that sin is really abolished in those to whom it is remitted, it does not follow on that account that remission itself consists in that abolition. The former is concerned only with the guilt of sin, the latter with its pollution; the former considers sin with its relation or obligation to punishment, the latter as a quality inherent in the subject; that is performed at the same time and at once, this little by little and successively. Nor does an infusion of righteousness forthwith follow remission of sin from the nature of the thing, as he who remits another's debt ought not at once to give a new sum of money to him. We pardon the sins of others, nor on that account do we expel them from them, since there is one action which is done concerning someone and about him objectively, another which is done in someone subjectively.

Second proposition: remission of sin is total and absolute with respect to guilt as well as to punishment. This is also against the Romanists, who urge a partial and not a total remission of guilt, but not of punishment; or of eternal, but not of temporal punishment. "If anyone says that after justification is received, criminality is so remitted to any penitent sinner and the guilt of eternal punishment destroyed, that no exposedness to temporal punishment to be taken away either in this world or in the future remains, before he can gain access into the kingdom of heaven, let him be accursed."

For guilt to be remitted while the punishment is not remitted is absurd (*asystaton*) because there is no punishment without guilt and remission of guilt is nothing else than deliverance from punishment. (2) It is repugnant to Scripture which nowhere speaks of the remission of sin except on the supposition that no punishment of it is exacted; otherwise a great disturbance would be introduced into the Scriptures and nothing could be considered fixed and certain in them. Also great darkness would be poured over both the divine promises and threatenings, as often as either remission of sin is promised or denied (whether it is only of the guilt or also of the punishment; and whether of all or of a certain part of each). Again, how could God be said to cast behind his back, not to impute, to destroy, not to remember, if he still exacts the punishment of them (i.e., recollects and imputes them to punishment)? (3) The common manner of speaking does not suffer it to be said that his sin has been remitted from whom some punishment of sin is exacted. For thus anyone might be said at the same time and at once "to let go" (*aphienai*) and "to keep hold" (*kratein*) of something (which is a contradiction); as no one would say that a debt had been remitted to a person from whom the payment of it is still required. (4) The nature of remission, which is entirely gratuitous, cannot allow this because what is obtained by the payment of any price, cannot be called gratuitous. (5) The justified cannot have peace with God according to Paul (Rom. 5:1), if they are still to be disturbed in life or after death. (6) In believers after the reception of justification, there is no condemnation (Rom. 8:1). Therefore no punishment remains, since condemnation is the devoting to punishment.

(7) This hypothesis supposes either that Christ has not fully satisfied for us or that God demands the payment of the same debt twice (both of which are impious and blasphemous). Nor can it be replied, "Subordinates are not at variance because the satisfactions of men depend upon Christ's satisfaction, and from it have the power of satisfying; that Christ satisfied immediately for the guilt and exposedness to eternal death, mediately, however, for temporal punishment also, inasmuch as he furnishes the grace by which we ourselves make satisfaction to God." (a) It is gratuitously supposed that our satisfactions can be subordinated to Christ's satisfaction, since they are expressly opposed to it. For if righteousness came by the law then Christ is dead in vain (Gal. 2:21). (b) This mediate satisfaction is unheard-of in Scripture, which never says that Christ satisfied that he might acquire for us the power to satisfy, but by himself (*di' heautou*) made expiation for sins, and thus reconciled us to God and freed us from the curse of the law, being made a curse for us. Now how could Christ be said to have borne our sins in his own body on the tree (i.e., their punishment) and to have freed us from the curse and to have blotted out and taken out of the way the handwriting which was against us (Col. 2:14) and by one offering to have perfected forever them that are sanctified (Heb. 10:14), if believers are still bound by the guilt of some punishments for which they are yet to make satisfaction? Finally, the mode of speaking does not suffer it to be said that he made satisfaction for us, unless he has cancelled our debt with his own money.

No less absurd is the answer "Our satisfactions are required that the satisfaction of Christ and the remission acquired by him may be applied to us." Although the satisfaction of Christ must be applied to particular believers to avail them, this ought to be done by the word and sacraments externally, by the Spirit and faith internally; but it cannot be done by satisfactions which ought to be offered to God, not to men. Nor have we ever heard it said that the remission of a debt is applied by an exaction of it and that this rests upon the debtor in order that he may enjoy the payment made for him by his security, so that the money which the sponsor paid for him, he also should pay out of his own funds to the creditor afterwards (or certainly some part of it). Again, if (in order that Christ's satisfaction for temporal punishments may be applied to us) our satisfactions are required, why are they not equally necessary in order that the same may be applied for guilt and eternal punishment? Or if they confess that they are not required for that application, why should they be required for the other, since no reason for the difference can be assigned? Finally, if Christ's satisfaction ought to be applied by our satisfaction, our satisfaction again would have to be applied by another satisfaction and so on to infinity.

What Scripture sometimes says of the exercise of judgment against the church and believers (1 Peter 4:17; 1 Cor. 11:32 and elsewhere) does not favor the error of the Romanists. The judgment of a vindictive judge is one thing; the judgment of paternal chastisement is another. The one is legal, the other evangelical; the one proceeding from wrath and hatred, the other from love and mercy; the one for destruction and death, the other for correction and salvation; the one is exercised against the wicked and rebels, the other towards the pious and believers, not to destroy, but to teach and make them more cautious afterwards. Hence Augustine says, "What you bewail is medicine, not a punishment; chastisement not condemnation; be unwilling to repel the rod, if you do not wish to be repelled from the inheritance." The former is incompatible (*asystaton*) with remission, not the latter.

Although afflictions of themselves and in their own nature are truly the punishment of sin according to the threatening of the law (Lev. 26), still on account of our gratuitous reconciliation with God in Christ they cease to be punishments (*timōriai*). They become either fatherly chastisement (1 Cor. 11:32; Heb. 12:8); or necessary evidences (*dokimasiai*) that we may be manifested to ourselves and to others (James 1:2–3); or witnesses (*martyria*) or testimonies concerning the truth of doctrine (Acts 5:41). On this account, they are reckoned even among the blessings of God (Ps. 94:12; Job 5:17; Phil. 1:29; Heb. 12:6–7). They are connected with joy (Acts 5:41; James 1:2; Heb. 12:11). They have glorying as an attendant (Rom. 5:2–3). Therefore if they are still called punishments after the remission of sin, this is not said properly because they are without the formal reason of punishment (to wit, that it should be inflicted from the wrath of the Judge as the avenging of sin and the destruction of the sinner). Rather it is said improperly, both because they were of themselves the punishments of sin and because they tend to the destruction of the flesh and of the old man.

This full and total remission of sins being established, the treasury of papal indulgences sinks and that most foul trafficking of the mystery of iniquity is swept away. For if the remission granted to believers is entire and total, freeing them from all guilt and punishment, why are necessary satisfactions further invented (either personal or another's) for the taking away of punishment, if not eternal at least temporal? I dismiss the various arguments, which prove not only the weakness but also the falsity of that error (concerning which we will speak in the proper place) from which it will appear that this comment is not only unwritten (*agraphon*), but also contrary to what is written (*antigraphon*) and unreasonable (*alogon*) and filled with innumerable contradictions and impieties. Hence it should not seem amazing if this occasioned (as is well known) the work of the Reformation in the year 1519 at Zurich by Zwingli; in the year

1517 at Wittenberg by Luther, who could not endure that most disgraceful traffic in sacred things.

Nor ought we to recur to the indulgences of the fathers, which have nothing in common with the modern papal indulgences (as they cannot be ignorant who have any knowledge of the ancient discipline). Since it is evident that in the ancient church very severe canonical punishments and satisfactions were imposed upon public sinners by penitential canons, specimens of which can be seen not only in the canons of the councils of Elvira, Ancyra and Nicea, but also in the decrees of Burchard, Ivo and Gratian (which were not rendered properly to God in the court of heaven as a satisfactory punishment for their sins, but only to the church itself for the extinction and reparation of the scandal by which it was injured). But since on account of that rigor many were reduced to desperation and relapsed into Gentilism, a modification of indulgences was introduced, which sinners obtained either by the intercession of martyrs or received from their bishops (their serious grief being regarded lest they should be swallowed up of sadness), by which, the severity being relaxed, they were restored to communion before the time required by the canons and a dispensation of canonical punishments was granted to them, as may be seen in Cyprian, *Letters* 15, 16, 17; Canons 5 and 11 of the Council of Nicea; Canons 21 and 22 of the Council of Ancyra (A.D. 314), and Canon 37 of the Council of Agathensis. Afterwards most persons withdrawing from the yoke of the penitential canons, partly changes and partly redemptions of canonical satisfactions were introduced. Hence a fast of three days was redeemed by a recitation of fifty psalms, and by the feeding of some destitute person, or by three denarii from him who did not know the psalms. This gate of redemptions, however, being once opened, the sale of indulgences at length began in the eleventh century under Urban II. To make them of great importance, various comments were devised concerning their value and efficacy, not only in the court of earth (as to canonical punishment), but also in the court of heaven and as to the satisfaction to be rendered to divine justice for sins. Hence it is evident how much these indulgences differ from the ancient, which were nothing else than relaxations of canonical punishments and dispensations from their severity for the consolation of private persons and the common edification of the church. However the modern are held to be relaxations of the satisfactory punishments of divine justice.

Third proposition: "Remission is extended to all the sins entirely of believers, of whatever kind they may be, future as well as past and present, but in their own order." This question is moved with regard to future sins—are they also remitted at the same time and at once with the past and present sins? For there are some even of our theologians of great reputation who think that in the justification of the sinner all his sins (the future equally with the past) are at the same time and at once remitted, both because the righteousness of Christ, which is the foundation of our justification, is wholly (however great it is) imputed at once and at the same time to us and because justification ought to leave no room for condemnation (Rom. 8:1). Nay, being justified, they have peace with God (Rom. 5:1) and are called blessed (Ps. 32:1). This could not be said if they could still be subjected to condemnation on account of future sins not remitted.

We think the difficulty can be overcome by a distinction. All sins (future as well as past) cannot be said to be remitted at the same time and once formally and explicitly because as they are not accidents of a nonentity, so as long as the sin is not, punishment is not due to it; and since it is not due, it cannot be remitted (as a debt not yet contracted cannot be cancelled). Besides for the remission of sin there is required a confession and repentance of it, which cannot be made unless it has been committed. Hence we are ordered to seek remission of sins every day, which is to be applied to sins committed, not to anticipate their perpetration. But because in justification the righteousness of Christ is applied to us (which is the foundation upon which the remission of all our sins rests) and because from the covenant of grace God promises that he will not remember our sins, nothing prevents us from saying that in this sense sins are remitted eminently and virtually because in the righteousness of Christ imputed to us is the foundation of that remission. And thus all our sins are remitted by God, whether past or present or future, but with respect to the time in which they are committed; so that past and present are actually remitted, the future when they are committed will most certainly be remitted according to God's promise. Thus the state of justification remaining undisturbed and the acceptation of the person remaining uninterrupted and the general remission of sins already committed, the following and future as to particular absolution are not actually pardoned before their commission; nay, before they have been repented of either generally or particularly.

I confess if we regard the eternal purpose of God in which all things, even the future, appeared to God as present (Acts 15:18) and the merit and acquisition of Christ, who offered to God a perfectly sufficient ransom (*lytron*) for the expiation of all our sins, so that as to the promise given by God in the covenant of grace concerning their remission, remission under this relation (*schesei*) can be said to be extended to all sins whether past or future. But if the actual remission itself is regarded, which is made by an intimation of the absolving sentence in the heart of the believer and penitent, it can be referred only to sins already committed. Thus to take away the guilt of subsequent sins, there is required a particular application of remission, not only as to the sense and assurance of remission, but also as to the true and real forgiveness itself.

As the person whose sins are pardoned can be considered, either as to the state of grace (in which he is constituted by justification) or as to the particular acts (which he can afterwards commit), so remission can be viewed in two aspects: either generally as to state (according to which God receives the believing and penitent sinner into grace on account of Christ and bestows upon him the pardon of all the sins of which he is guilty); or specially as to particular acts of sin into which he afterwards falls, for taking away the guilt of which a particular absolution is needed. Not that the state of justification into which he is translated can be dissolved or remission once bestowed be abrogated, because God remains always his Father, but a Father angry on account of sins recently committed (which although they cannot constitute him a "child of wrath" on account of the immutability of calling and justification, still they make him a "child under wrath," so that he deservedly incurs the fatherly indignation of God and has need forthwith of a new justification or particular remission of these sins through faith and repentance).

Although the justified believer has not as yet the formal remission of future sins, he does not cease to be happy and free from actual condemnation because he has the foundation from which he can infer with positive certainty that it is prepared for him according to God's promise. If the whole righteousness of Christ is at the same time imputed, its entire fruit does not flow out to us at once, but successively in proportion to the inrushings of sin (for the remission of which the believer ought to apply that ransom [lytron] to himself every day).

# 6

# ADOPTION

*What is the adoption which is given to us in justification?*

The other part of justification is adoption or the bestowal of a right to life, flowing from Christ's righteousness, which acquired for us not only deliverance from death, but also a right to life by the adoption with which he endows us. For on this account, he is said to have been made under the law (*hypo nomon*) by an economical subjection that he might redeem us from the bondage of the law and confer upon us the adoption or the right of sons (Gal. 4:4–5). On this, the right to life depends because "if children, then heirs" (Rom. 8:17). John says "to them who received him," i.e., "who believed on his name, he gave power to become the sons of God" (1:12). Here *exousia* does not signify authority or power because it has reference here to inferiors; nor faculty or potency by which a person can make himself a son. Rather it signifies *axiōma* (i.e., the dignity and right of sons).

However adoption here is not taken by us (as it is elsewhere) for an external calling and reception into the covenant (such as was formerly the case with the Jews, whose is said to be the adoption, Rom. 9:4). Nor for the sense and use of adoption which is made by emancipation, such as belongs to believers of the New Testament, who because they are made adults and are no longer minors are said to have received the Spirit of adoption and are no longer called servants, nor are held in the manner of servants, but are sons and heirs who rejoice in this right (Gal. 4:5). Nor for the full manifestation of adoption, which will occur in the resurrection. In this sense, believers are said to wait for the adoption (i.e., the resurrection of their bodies, Rom. 8:23). Rather it is taken for a juridical act of God by which from his mere mercy, he adopts into his family through faith in Christ those whom he elected to salvation from eternity and bestows upon them the name and right of sons as to inheritance.

However as the word "adoption" is derived from a custom received among men, so the action itself has a multiple analogy with civil adoption (although it differs also in various things and is better). Adoption is defined by lawyers as a "lawful act imitating nature introduced for the consolation of those who have no children." Thus there is required here: first an adopter, who can have the authority of a father who (destitute of children) supplies the defect of nature by law and receives a stranger into his own family and promises to him paternal favor; (2) the person adopted, who passes from his father's family into another and (his state being changed) changes his name and life and has a right to the paternal goods and especially to the inheritance; and in turn binds himself to all the duties of filial obedience. Thus in this matter, adoption is not an act of nature, but of a gracious will which our heavenly Father wished to exercise towards us. In this sense, he is said "to have begotten us of his own will" (James 1:18) and the very name adoption (*hyiothesias*) denotes this voluntary and most free disposition of God. By it God transfers us strangers and foreigners (who were the servants or slaves of Satan) from the family of the old Adam and the power of darkness and admits us into his own family and the kingdom of light and gives us the dignity of sons. He not only bestows upon us the glorious name of dearly beloved sons (1 John 3:1; Rev. 2:17; 3:12) with the distinctions and honors pertaining to them, but also gives us a right to all his goods of grace as well as of glory. All this comes under the name of inheritance as acquired not by any merit, but given by the mere grace of the Father to us in virtue of our adoption by him. And we in turn (answering by faith to this great love) bind ourselves to filial worship and obedience to him (2 Cor. 6:18; 1 Peter 1:15–16; Mal. 1:6, 8).

Of whatever kind may be the analogy, still a great and remarkable difference always intervenes. For what the law does among men, this is a work of mere good will (*eudokias*). That was sought out for the solace of childlessness to supply a defect of nature; but this was made for our consolation only, not for God's, who was perfectly well pleased with his only begotten Son. That was ordained for the succession to the goods of a deceased father, but this only for a participation in the goods of a Father living forever. That can give the name, the titles and distinctions of sons, but not the mind and qualities. But in this, God by adopting changes the heart, and to whom he gratuitously gives the right of sons, he also impresses upon them the mind and character of sons by the Spirit of adoption. That does not make them good, but supposes them to be so; for neither would a man adopt anyone as a son unless he perceived in him something lovely. But this is a work of mere grace which does not suppose anything good in us who were enemies, rebels and most corrupt. Thus God adopts us, not because we are good, but to make us good.

Here belongs the testamentary disposition which the Father is said to have instituted for giving us the inheritance. It is nothing else than the final and immutable will sealed in the Scriptures and confirmed by the blood and death of Christ, by which he pronounces elect believers his heirs. Christ clearly intimates this: "I appoint" (*diatithemai*, or give by a will) "unto you a kingdom, as my Father hath appointed (*dietheto*) unto me" (Luke 22:29). "And for this cause he is the mediator of the new testament," says Paul, "that by means of death, for the redemption of the transgressions that were under the first testament, they which are called might receive the promise of eternal inheritance" (Heb. 9:15). The goods left by this testament do not pertain only to "the inheritance of this world" (Rom. 4:13), according to which all things are ours (1 Cor. 3:21), but it is especially the inheritance of heaven or of the kingdom of heaven (Matt. 25; James 2:5). Thus it is the inheritance of God himself, who (as he is the highest good) is often called our portion and inheritance (Gen. 15:1; Ps. 16:5; Jer. 10:16), as believers are the portion and inheritance of God (Ps. 33:12).

Now although this privilege as to the thing is common to all the believers of the Old Testament, no less than to those of the New, who were both sons of God and had a right to the heavenly inheritance (to which after death they were admitted), still it is certain that the condition of believers of the New Testament as to the mode is far better in this respect: they are no longer in an infantile age, held like slaves under teachers and the rudiments of the world, when they were not able to have either the sense or the use of their right, animated by the spirit of bondage. But now being adults and emancipated by Christ, they are admitted to the sanctuary of the Father and have a full sense and fruit of their right, the Spirit of adoption being received, in virtue of which they can confidently cry out, Abba, Father. Paul refers to this when he says, "Christ was made under the law, to redeem them that were under the law" (to wit, under the curse of the moral law and under the yoke of the ceremonial law) "that we might receive the adoption of sons" (Gal. 4:4–5). Not that only by which we are separated from the children of wrath and of the Devil, but also that by which we far excel infants, who do not differ from slaves.

From these positions, it is gathered that to no purpose do some anxiously ask here how justification and adoption differ from each other, and whether adoption is by nature prior to justification (as some hold, who think it is the first and immediate fruit of faith by which we are united and joined to Christ; or whether posterior to and consequent upon it, as others). For since it is evident from what has been said that justification is a benefit by which God (being reconciled to us in Christ) absolves us from the guilt of sins and gives us a right to life, it follows that adoption is included in justification itself as a part which, with the remission of sins, constitutes the whole of this benefit. Nor can it be distinguished from the adoption except inasmuch as it is taken strictly for remission of sins, since in its formal conception it includes also acceptation to life, which flows from the imputation of Christ's righteousness.

Nor is adoption here to be confounded with our union with Christ. For although it necessarily flows from it as its cause and foundation (since from union with Christ depends the communion of all his benefits, of justification and of sanctification and of glory), still it cannot (if we wish to speak accurately) be identified with it. Rather it stands related to it as an effect to its cause. Hence it is that, being united to Christ as our head and the first-begotten of God, his most perfect righteousness becomes ours by the imputation of God and the reception of faith, upon which depend both absolution from sins and the adoption or acceptation to life and the inheritance which is the right of sons. For as many as obtain that dignity are not only received into God's family to be members of his house (Gal. 6:10), to be always under the fatherly protection of God, depending upon him for nutrition, education and perpetual conservation, but have a right to the inheritance (Rom. 8:17), i.e., the possession of all the goods of the Father and the enjoyment of God himself (which is our inheritance).

From this adoption springs Christian liberty, which is not an immunity from all laws (divine and human) and a license to live according to our pleasure and to indulge the lusts of the flesh (as the Libertines profess, changing liberty into licentiousness); not an exemption from the civil obligation of subjection and from the tributes and jurisdiction of magistrates (as the various Anabaptists maintain and which the Romish clergy claim for themselves against the express teachings of Scripture); but it is a spiritual and mystical manumission obtained for us by the blood of Christ, by which from the spiritual bondage of the law, of sin, of the world and Satan (by whose chains we were before bound), we are brought into the liberty of the sons of God (as it is treated in John 8:32; 36; Rom. 6:15, 22; 8:2–3; Gal. 3:13; 4:6, 26; 5:1; Heb. 2:15 and elsewhere); through which being called into fellowship with God (as our Father) and with Christ (as our brother), we obtain dominion over the creatures and are heirs of the kingdom of Heaven.

# THE JUSTIFICATION OF FAITH

*Does faith justify us properly and by itself or only relatively and instrumentally? The former we deny; the latter we affirm against the Socinians, Remonstrants and Romanists.*

Since justification can be viewed either actively (on the part of God who justifies) or passively (on the part of man who is justified), a twofold handling of it can also be adopted: either with respect to the benefit itself conferred upon us by God and of the righteousness imputed to us; or with respect to its reception and application made by faith (of which we now treat).

However, it is not controverted whether faith justifies—for Scripture so clearly asserts this that no one dares to deny it. Rather we inquire regarding the manner in which it justifies, in describing which there is an amazing discrepancy of opinions.

All our opponents agree in this—that faith justifies properly and by itself and so is our very righteousness—but with some differences. For the Socinians maintain that faith or the act of believing is the cause of our justification so that there is no other immediate and formal righteousness by which we are just before God than our faith; also justification is a universal affection of faith—"Not because it is considered such by the gracious acceptation of God; by which it pleased him to reckon faith for perfect righteousness, or for a perfect fulfillment of the law, no otherwise than formally under the legal covenant, the perfect obedience of the law was that universal righteousness upon which life depended" (as Socinus frequently expresses it). The Remonstrants agree with them on this point in their Confession.

The Romanists hold that faith is the disposing and cause *sine qua non*, which not only disposes to righteousness, but also begins and merits righteousness itself. "If anyone says that the wicked are justified by faith alone, so that he understands nothing else to be required to cooperate for obtaining the grace of justification and is necessary from no part, to be prepared and disposed with the motion of his own will, let him be accursed." Bellarmine says, "Faith justifies as the beginning and root of justification because it is the first motion towards God, for it behooves one approaching God to believe that God is." This opinion is founded upon a false hypothesis—as if justification consists in an infusion of righteousness and is a certain physical motion which demands previous dispositions in the subject before the introduction of the form.

However the orthodox differ wholly from them. They teach that faith is the organic and instrumental cause of our justification and that justification is ascribed to it, not properly and by itself (inasmuch as it is a work or as if it was the righteousness itself by which we are justified before God; or as if by its own worth or by the indulgence of God it deserves justification in whole or in part), but improperly and metonymically (inasmuch as Christ's righteousness, which faith apprehends, is the foundation and meritorious cause on account of which we are justified). So that it is said to justify relatively and organically: relatively because the object of faith is our true righteousness before God; organically because faith is the instrument for receiving on our part and for applying to ourselves, that righteousness.

Two things therefore must be done by us here. First, negatively (*kat' arsin*) the false mode of the justification of faith (introduced by the Socinians and Romanists) must be removed. Second, affirmatively (*kata thesin*) the true and genuine sense must be established. As to the former, faith or the act of believing is not considered as our righteousness with God by a gracious acceptation: (a) because what is only the instrument for receiving righteousness cannot be our righteousness itself formally. Now faith holds here only the relation (*scheisn*) of an instrument, as is evident both from its proper act (which is instrumental and consists in the reception of Christ [John 1:12] and the acceptance of righteousness [Rom. 5:17] and of the remission of sins [Acts 26:18]); and from the subordination of the causes of justification to the same effect (to wit, the grace of God, the redemption of Christ and faith). This is alluded to by Paul in Rom. 3:24 where faith cannot sustain any other meaning than that of an instrument, since the grace of God holds the relation of an efficient principle and the redemption of Christ that of the meritorious cause.

(b) Because faith is distinguished from the righteousness itself which is imputed to us, both because it is said to be "of faith" and "by faith" (Rom. 1:17; 3:22; Phil. 3:9) and because Christ with his obedience and satisfaction is that righteousness which is imputed to us (Isa. 53:11; Jer. 23:6; 1 Cor. 1:30; 2 Cor. 5:21; Gal. 3:13–14), which faith indeed apprehends as its object, but with which it cannot be identified. Hence Scripture nowhere says that God willed to count our faith for righteousness, but that he made Christ unto us righteousness; that he is Jehovah our righteousness and that we are the righteousness of God in him.

(c) Because we are not justified except by a perfect righteousness. For we have to deal with the strict justice of God, which cannot be deceived. Now no faith here is perfect. Nor can it be said that it is not indeed a perfect righteousness of itself, but is admitted as such by God and considered such by a gratuitous lowering of the law's demands. For in the court of divine justice (which demands an adequate and absolutely perfect payment), there cannot be room for a gracious acceptation which is an imaginary payment. Again, since our justification is a forensic and judicial act (where God shows himself just, Rom. 3:25), it does not admit of a gracious acceptation (which never proceeds from the authority and sentence of the Judge, but from the voluntary and private stipulation of the parties).

(d) If faith is counted for righteousness, we will be justified by works because thus faith cannot but have the relation of a work which justifies. And yet it is clear that in this business Paul always opposes faith to works as incompatible (*asystata*) and two antagonistic (*antidiērēmena*) means by which man is justified either by his own obedience and in himself, by the law, or by another's obedience by the gospel. Nor does the difference between these modes of justification consist in this—that in the former a perfect obedience and in the latter an imperfect is accepted of God as perfect, since the mode of justification would be always the same—by works. Rather the difference consists in this—that since in both cases a perfect righteousness is required, in the former from the strictness (*akribodikaiō*) of the law God demands a personal righteousness, here from the forbearance (*epieikeia*) of the gospel he admits another's (to wit, the righteousness of Christ). Thus faith cannot be said to justify properly and by itself unless we slide back to the old covenant and return to legal justification.

"The faith of Abraham," it is said, "was imputed to him for righteousness" (Gen. 15:6; Rom. 4:3). Not properly because in this way he would have been justified by works (which the apostle denies in the same place). But (1) relatively and metonymically, so that faith is taken for its object (Gal. 3:25), i.e., for that which faith believes (to wit, that the promise concerning the seed [from Gal. 3:16], not so much bodily as spiritual, which he received by faith, was the foundation of his justification). This is confirmed by the circumstance that what does not inhere and what is contradistinguished from works is here said to be imputed. Thus in this sense faith is said to be imputed for righteousness by a hypallage because righteousness is imputed by faith, as the apostle declares in equivalent terms (Gal. 3:5–6; Rom. 3:22). Nor is this to wrest the Scriptures and to express coldly the power and efficacy of faith, as Forbes falsely charges upon our theologians. Nay, no more clearly and truly can the genuine sense of that imputation be set forth. For since that thing which is imputed to us for righteousness ought to be our righteousness before God (i.e., that on account of which God justifies us); nor can faith be that (as we have already said and as he himself does not deny when he recognizes it to be the instrumental cause); it is clear that this phrase cannot be taken properly, but only metonymically with regard to the object. Nor is anything more usual in Scripture than for a faculty to be taken for its object. This does not prevent (2) faith from being said to be imputed for righteousness organically because it is the instrumental cause which apprehends the righteousness of Christ by a metonymy of the effect for the efficient, as it is elsewhere called eternal life (John 17:3; 12:50), i.e., the instrumental cause of life.

In vain, however, does Arminius contend that the righteousness of Christ is not imputed for righteousness, since it is that very righteousness itself (to wit, supposing that is not properly righteousness which is imputed to us for righteousness). He falsely confounds to impute for righteousness by gracious acceptation that which is not a righteousness, and to impute to a person for righteousness that which he did not have. The first sense has no place here, only the latter. Accordingly what Abraham had not is said to be imputed to him for righteousness and the righteousness of Christ is imputed to us (i.e., reckoned ours), which was not ours. Thus imputation does not deny the truth of the thing or the perfection of the righteousness, but only the truth of the possession by ascribing to a person what was not properly his.

What is said concerning anyone in Scripture ought to be altogether in him, but according to the manner which it teaches itself. Now the manner in which justification and salvation are ascribed to faith, does not consist in its own proper efficiency (as if our faith wrought or effected them), but they are placed only in its fiducial apprehension and the application. Nor otherwise are we said to please God by faith (Heb. 11:6) and to be purged of sin (Acts 15:9), than because it applies to us the righteousness and blood of Christ, who purges us from sins and makes us acceptable to God.

It is one thing for blessings to be conferred according to faith (i.e., under the condition of faith) under which they are promised in the word and which we acknowledge with the Scriptures; another for faith to justify properly and by itself or to count faith itself for righteousness and thus to impute it for righteousness to the believer. There faith holds the relation of an instrument. Here, however, it holds that of a principal cause and foundation (which we deny).

Second, against the Romanists we prove that faith does not justify dispositively or meritoriously, as the beginning and root of righteousness. (1) The Holy Spirit nowhere ascribes to faith the beginning or only a part of disposition to justification, but the whole and entire justification. (2) Thus the antithesis of the apostle between works and faith would not hold good, since faith would always justify like a work. (3) Justification, as being a forensic act, takes place at once and in a moment (*en atom\o*); nor can it admit of a beginning and progress. (4) Thus we could be said to be justified "on account of faith" (*dia tēn pistin*). The Scripture never says this, but always either "by faith" (*pistei*) or "through faith" (*dia tēs pisteōs, ek pisteōs*) as by an instrument. If in various passages these prepositions—"by" and "through"—have a causality properly so called (as when they are connected with the death and blood of Christ), it does not follow that they have the same force when used concerning the justification of faith. Nay, since it is evident that a man cannot be justified by two righteousnesses (one in himself, the other in Christ), if the righteousness and blood of Christ is the proper cause of his justification, this cannot be ascribed to faith, but only the instrumental cause. (5) This opinion falsely supposes that justification is a physical motion inhering in the subject, which needs previous dispositions by which it may be acquired so as to be introduced into the subject. But this is false since it is a forensic act (as was proved before) to which man holds himself objectively, not subjectively. And although faith is required on the part of man for receiving this benefit, it does not follow that it has the relation of a disposition by which the sinner is disposed to the infusion of righteousness.

Faith is viewed in different lights: either in the act itself of justification or in the person of the justified or in the effect of justification. In the person of the justified, it is well called "the beginning of righteousness"; not imputed but inherent because it is the root of all virtues. Thus in the effect of justification, it is the principle and cause of new obedience; but in the act of justification, it can be nothing else than an instrument apprehending and applying to man that which justifies. Thus he is justified not by the merit of faith, but only by it as a means.

Although justification is drawn away from works as to merit and a properly so-called efficiency, it does not follow that the same is ascribed to faith in the same manner. Nay, because it is taken away from works, it cannot for the same reason be ascribed to faith because it would thus justify as a work; nor could we be said to be justified without works. It therefore suffices (in order to save the opposition of the apostle) that faith should be substituted by him in the place of works because by faith we most surely obtain what the Jews in vain sought in works (although it acts here not meritoriously, but only instrumentally).

Faith is said to save us (Luke 7:50), not by meriting something in order to justification, but only receptively and organically because it was the instrument receptive of that benefit. Nothing is more frequent than by a metalepsis to ascribe to an instrument the effect of the principal cause (as when "the gospel" is said "to be the power of God unto salvation," Rom. 1:16; the diligent hand is said to increase the house; the plough to enrich the farmer; the hand of the giver to relieve the poor; and the like). If elsewhere the greatness of the faith of the Canaanite woman to whom Christ granted the sought-for blessing is extolled (Matt. 15:28), its merit and efficiency is not on that account denoted. Believing, she was certainly healed because, faith being the medium, God bestowed this blessing upon her; but believing, he healed her, not on account of the fact that faith properly speaking effected or merited the healing.

Therefore the true mode of the justification of faith is no other than instrumental. (1) Its proper act consists in the reception of Christ and his righteousness, as was said before. (2) It justifies in no other manner than by its being directed to the death and obedience of Christ (to wit, by apprehending and applying Christ to itself as a ransom [*antilytron*] given for us and a propitiation [*hilasmon*] for sin, 1 John 2:2). (3) Faith in the Scriptures is described by "eating," "looking" and "touching," which have only an instrumental causality, not a proper efficiency (as the looking at a serpent did not cure per se, but relatively to the brazen serpent; nor does eating nourish except by food thrown into the mouth). (4) Justifying faith stands related in no other way to justification than as the faith of miracles stands related to the working of miracles; not effectively, but organically by apprehending the special promise given concerning them.

Not without reason, however, is this ascribed above all other things to the believer because it alone of all the virtues can subsist with grace as consisting in the mere reception and apprehension of an object placed beyond itself. Hence it is said to be "of faith, that it might be by grace" (Rom. 4:16), to wit, as man owes this entire blessing to God, he has no reason for glorying in himself. For if he were justified by works or inherent righteousness, he would seem to have something in which to glory; but when he is justified by faith (which gives nothing to God, but only receives) all glorying is excluded. This Toletus well explains when he gives the reason why the Scripture ascribes justification to faith alone: "Namely, because in faith it is more manifested that man is justified not by his own virtue, but by the merit of Christ. For as in beholding the serpent God placed healing in the desert, because the looking indicated more that the men were healed by the virtue of the serpent, not of any personal work or medicine; so faith shows that sinners are justified by the virtue and merit of Christ, in whom believing they are saved, not by any virtue and merit of their own. And it is the reason why justification is ascribed to faith especially by Paul, who strives to exclude from justification the works of the law, and human merit or efficacy, and to place it in the virtue and merit of Christ alone. Therefore he makes mention of faith in Christ. This neither repentance, nor love, nor hope have, for faith is carried more immediately and distinctly to it, by whose virtue we are justified."

Although the sacraments are external means and instruments applying (on the part of God) the promise of grace and justification, this does not hinder faith from being called the internal instrument and means on the part of man for receiving this benefit offered in the word and sealed by the sacraments.

What justifies as an instrument does not forthwith justify as a work, although that instrument is a work. It is one thing for it to be a work and another to justify as a work. What justifies as a work ought to be the meritorious cause of justification, but what justifies as an instrument does not justify meritoriously, but only apprehensively and receptively; not by giving, but by receiving. Therefore the action of faith justifies us, but not as an action simply (as it were our righteousness with God), but in relation to its object inasmuch as it receives Christ. As the extension of the beggar's hand is indeed the act of the beggar prescribed by the rich man, still as an act it does not enrich the beggar, but insofar as in this way he applies the gift of the rich man to himself and makes it his own.

Although faith is called "the work of God" (John 6:29), it does not follow that it justifies as a work. Although it is enjoined by God (and in this sense is called the work of God and is due from man that he may obtain life), it is not on this account due as the meritorious cause of that life, but only as a means and instrument receptive of the righteousness of Christ, which is the true cause of life. And thus it is so called by Christ imitatively (*mimētikōs*) and by allusion to the Jewish sense, who sought life by the works of the law: "What must we do," said they, "that we may work the works of God?" To this legal question Jesus answers, not legally, but evangelically (yet in a legal style, taking the legal phrase from the expression of the Jews and applying it to his discourse): "This is the work of God that ye believe"—intimating that no further work was necessary to acquire salvation, but that faith was substituted in the place of all works for the reception of it (as if he said, work earnestly, only believe—this is work, this is labor). Evidently as to a sick man seeking by what medicine he is about to be healed, if the physician answers, this is the medicine which I prescribe to you; keep quiet and confide in me—he does not wish to intimate that that rest and confidence are any remedies to cure him, but he means only this—there is no need of medicine. Thus the Scripture often ascribes the names of things (to which men attribute falsely a great efficacy and value) to those things which are truly efficacious and valuable; as the gospel is called law because what the law sought, the gospel gives; what the Jews vainly sought in the law is obtained by the gospel. Thus regeneration is called circumcision (Phil. 3:3); believers are called sons of Abraham; love and piety are called fasting (Isa. 58:6–7); and faith is called a work.

But we think it ought not to be anxiously inquired whether faith stands here in the relation of an instrument or also of a condition, as some think. Both may be ascribed to it, provided the condition is not understood as that in view of which God justifies man in the legal covenant. For in this sense, it cannot be called a condition, unless we agree with the Socinians and Remonstrants, who hold that faith or the act of believing is admitted by God by a gracious accepta-

tion for a perfect righteousness (which we have just now re-
futed). Rather it is taken broadly for all that is required on
our part to obtain this benefit—whether it has the relation
of a cause properly so called or only instrumental. For thus
as that condition has the relation (*schesin*) of an instrument,
so the instrument has the relation of a condition on our part
without which justification cannot be granted. Moreover
concerning the manner in which faith concurs to justification and concerning its threefold act—dispository, justifaca-
tory and consolatory.

# 8

# JUSTIFICATION BY FAITH ALONE

*Does faith alone justify? We affirm against the Romanists.*

This question also lies between us and the Romanists, who not only corrupt the true mode of the justification of faith by making the instrumental cause meritorious or at least dispositive, but by connecting with it the other virtues both as attendants and companions in this act. Hence arose the controversy concerning "faith alone justifying" (*sole Fide Justificante*), which as it is of no less importance than the preceding, so it is agitated with no less warmth of spirit.

This question is not of recent birth. Even from the very beginning of the Christian religion, this was asserted by the false apostles of Judaizing Christians. They did not with full front attack the faith as the Pharisees, but on the side by a deadly mixture associating the law with the gospel, Moses with Christ and faith with works in the matter of justification, so that man should be justified not by faith alone, but at the same time by works also. Against them the apostle disputes in his epistles to the Galatians, Philippians and

Colossians. This is urged by the Romanists of this day, who hold that with faith, fear, hope, love, penitence, the purpose of a new life concurs to justification. "If anyone shall say that the wicked are justified by faith alone, so as to understand that nothing else is required to cooperate for the obtainment of the grace of justification and is necessary from no part, that he should be prepared and disposed by a motion of his own will, let him be accursed." This is more fully set forth in chapters 5 and 6, where the mode and necessity of preparation for justification are treated.

But that the state of the question may be the more easily understood, we must remark that a twofold trial can be entered into by God with man: either by the law (inasmuch as he is viewed as guilty of violating the law by sin and thus comes under the accusation and condemnation of the law); or by the gospel (inasmuch as he is accused by Satan of having violated the gospel covenant and so is supposed to be an unbeliever and impenitent or a hypocrite, who has not testified by works the faith he has professed with his mouth). Now to this twofold trial a twofold justification ought to answer; not in the Romish sense, but in a very different sense. The first is that by which man is absolved from the guilt of sin on account of the righteousness of Christ imputed to us and apprehended by faith; the other is that by which he is freed from the charge of unbelief and hypocrisy and declared to be a true believer and child of God; one who has fulfilled the gospel covenant (if not perfectly as to degree, still sincerely as to parts) and answered to the divine call by the exercise of faith and piety. The first is justification properly so called; the other is only a declaration of it. That is justification of cause *a priori*; this is justification of sign or of effect *a posteriori*, declaratively. In that, faith alone can have a place because it alone apprehends the righteousness of Christ, by whose merit we are freed from the condemnation of the law; in this, works also are required as the effects and signs of faith, by which its truth and sincerity are declared against the accusation of unbelief and hypocrisy. For as faith justifies a person, so works justify faith.

The question does not concern justification *a posteriori* and declaratively in the fatherly and gospel trial—whether faith alone without works concurs to it (for we confess that works come in here with faith; yea, that works only are properly regarded because it is concerned with the justification of faith, which can be gathered from no other source more certainly than by works as its effects and indubitable proofs). Rather the question concerns justification *a priori*, which frees us from the legal trial, which is concerned with the justification of the wicked and the perfect righteousness, which can be opposed to the curse of the law and acquire for us a right to life—whether works come into consideration here with faith (as the Romanists hold) or whether faith alone (as we maintain).

(2) The question is not whether faith alone justifies to the exclusion either of the grace of God or the righteousness of Christ or the word and sacraments (by which the blessing of justification is presented and sealed to us on the part of God), which we maintain are necessarily required here; but only to the exclusion of every other virtue and habit on our part. Hence the Romanists have no reason for accusing us of confusion (*akatastasias*) in this argument as if we ascribed justification at one time to the grace of God, at another to the blood of Christ and then again to faith. For all these as they are mutually subordinated in a different class of cause, consist with each other in the highest degree.

(3) The question is not whether solitary faith (i.e., separated from the other virtues) justifies (which we grant could not easily be the case, since it is not even true and living faith); but whether it "alone" (*sola*) concurs to the act of jus-

tification (which we assert); as the eye alone sees, but not when torn out of the body. Thus the particle "alone" (*sola*) does not determine the subject, but the predicate (i.e., "faith only does not justify" [*sola fides non justificat*], but "faith justifies alone" [*fides justificat sola*]. The coexistence of love in him who is justified is not denied; but its coefficiency or co-operation in justification is denied. (4) The question is not whether the faith "which justifies" (*quae justificat*) works by love (for otherwise it would not be living but dead); rather the question is whether faith "by which it justifies" (*qua justificat*) or in the act itself of justification, is to be considered under such a relation (*schesei*) (which we deny).

Hence the question returns to this—Does faith justify, not as it is objectively the doctrine of salvation, but subjectively as it assents to that saving doctrine and applies it to itself; not as the promise to do something, but as we rest upon the promises in Christ as sufficient; alone (*sola*), not by reason of existence (i.e., solitary without faith and love), but in respect to function or efficiency; not by way of preparation with other virtues or of merit, but relatively after the manner of an instrument, apprehending the satisfaction of Christ and fiducially applying it. The Romanists deny; we assert.

First, man is justified by faith without works; therefore by faith alone. The reason of the consequence is manifest because there are not more modes of justifying than these two—by faith and by works. Thus, one being removed, the other must not only necessarily be left, but also left alone. Otherwise the enumeration would not be legitimate. Now why would the apostle so often and so expressly institute an antithesis between faith and works in this matter, if works could concur with faith in any way to the act of justification? Would he not in this particular have occasioned believers to err by removing works absolutely and simply from it, if they contribute anything towards it? Let the various passages in which exclusives are employed be carefully examined and the thing will be clearer than the midday sun: "We conclude that a man is justified by faith without the deeds of the law" (Rom. 3:28); "By grace are ye saved, through faith; and that not of yourselves: it is the gift of God: not of works" (Eph. 2:8); and more clearly, "knowing that a man is not justified by the works of the law, but by the faith [ean mē dia pisteōs] of Jesus Christ" (Gal. 2:16). Here it is certain that the particle (eimē) is adversative and exclusive (as often elsewhere, Matt. 12:4; 24:36; Mark 13:32; John 17:12; Rev. 9:4; 21:27) from the force of the immediate opposition of faith and works, which mutually displace each other. Nor can the Romanists themselves deny this. Estius says the most learned interpreters follow this opinion (which Salmeron, Justiniani and others confirm). To no purpose, therefore, do others pretend that ean mē is here exceptive, with the meaning that a man is not justified by works, except as faith in Christ approaches to works. This is the very thing which Paul opposes against the false apostles, who maintained that not works alone could justify a man, but faith mingled with works (so that justification might be ascribed partly to faith and partly to works, which Paul frequently asserts is inconsistent [asystaton]—as Salmeron and Estius acknowledge). No better is the explanation of Cornelius a Lapide, who thinks that only the works of the law are excluded here, but not the works of hope, fear and love, which faith begets and produces, and which are under faith as daughters under a mother. We have seen above that all works are entirely excluded by Paul; not only the ceremonial, but also moral; not only those performed before grace, but also those performed from grace in the renewed.

Second, by that alone are we justified by which the righteousness of Christ is applied to us, who satisfied the law for us. Now this is done by faith alone; nor does it belong to love or to hope. Not to hope, which does not apprehend, but expects the thing promised. Not to love, which is concerned with the fulfillment of a command, not with the apprehension of a promise.

Third, we also are justified in the same way in which Abraham, the father of believers, was justified because what was written concerning him pertains not only to him, but to us also (Rom. 4:24). And yet Abraham was justified by faith alone: "Abraham believed in the Lord; and he counted it to him for righteousness" (Gen. 15:6), not of debt, on account of works preceding faith or subsequent to it, but of grace so that he might not have wherein to glory. For if "Abraham were justified by works, he hath whereof to glory; but not before God" (Rom. 4:2), to wit, he has no matter for glorying (*kauchēma*) (which is to be drawn from the preceding verses). The argument is from the destruction of the consequent to the destruction of the antecedent. If Abraham was justified by works, he hath whereof to glory in himself as if he had contributed something of his own to which a reward was due in the judgment of God. And yet he hath not whereof he can glory in himself before God. Therefore he was not justified by works. Nor can it be said here that works preceding faith are excluded; not those done from faith on account of which he could have had glory before God, as he is called a friend of God. For this is to gainsay openly and to contradict Paul to his face, who expressly testifies that Abraham had not whereof to glory before God. For it is gratuitously and most falsely supposed that only works antecedent to faith are excluded. But he excludes all works entirely without distinction and indeed the works of Abraham not only as an unbeliever, but also a believer (since this was said of him when he was already a believer and renewed). Again, he excludes all debt (v. 4); therefore, he also excludes every work. Finally, if he had not wished to exclude works done from faith, he ought not to have opposed "one working" to "one believing" simply, but one working without faith to one working from faith (which, however, he nowhere does).

Fourth, we are justified gratuitously and by the grace of God; therefore by faith alone because faith alone can consist with grace (Rom. 3:24–25). Nor is Bellarmine to be listened to, who wishes the particle "freely" not to exclude merits absolutely, but proper merits (or those which are from us, not from God). For merits arising from prevenient grace (which are called by them merits of congruity) are not opposed to grace, unless we wish grace to contend with grace. Nor does it follow hence that a man who is justified freely is justified by faith alone because as gratuitous justification does not exclude faith (because it is by grace), so neither ought it to exclude repentance and love, which are from grace. For as we have already remarked, the particle "freely" excludes entirely all merits; for whatever is freely given, that is acquired by no merit. Nor can the grace which is undue subsist with merit, which makes the pay due: "If by grace, then it is no more of works: otherwise grace is no more grace. But if it be of works, then it is no more grace: otherwise work is no more work" (Rom. 11:6). Now although faith is not excluded in justification, it is not on that account excluded from grace (for thus works done from grace would not have to be excluded). But because it alone above other virtues has a power receptive of and applicatory to the righteousness of Christ (and so supposes man to be a sinner and destitute of all righteousness), it excludes all merit.

Fifth, "the righteousness of God is said to be revealed from faith to faith; as it is written, The just shall live by faith" (Rom. 1:17). Here the apostle intends to prove that the gospel is the power of God (i.e., the sole most efficacious instrument for salvation) in opposition to the weakness of the law (Rom.

8:3; Heb. 7:19) because in it is the righteousness of God—not formally and subjectively (which is in God), but effectively (which is given to us by God); not inherent, because it is said to be manifested without the law by faith (Rom. 3:21), and to be imputed without works (Rom. 4:6), but imputed (which is opposed to man's righteousness and his own works, Rom. 10:3–4; Phil. 3:9). Thus the most perfect righteousness of Christ (which alone can bear the scrutiny of the divine trial as being divine and infinite, which is the cause and foundation of life and salvation) is revealed from faith to faith (i.e., is announced by the gospel, so as to be apprehended by faith alone because nothing besides faith can concur in the reception of it). Hence he does not say "from faith to works," but "from faith to faith" so that to faith alone this office is wholly ascribed. That Paul may prove this doctrine to be neither absurd nor new, he confirms it by the prophecy of Habakkuk where he says, "The just shall live by his faith" (2:4). Now although this prophecy refers also to a temporal blessing (viz., deliverance from the Babylonian captivity, which they would obtain by the intervention of faith in the divine promise; hence it is referred to by Paul in Heb. 10:38 to support believers in afflictions), still because the declaration of the prophet is general concerning faith in the promises of God, it is rightly applied specially to faith in Christ; and on this account the more—that the prophets and pious Jews regarded the promise of the Messiah as the foundation of all promises. Hence Paul (as best knowing the mind of the Holy Spirit) refers it (in Gal. 3:11 and in this place) to justification in order to teach that by faith alone man obtains the righteousness which brings eternal life to him. "The just shall live by faith," whether the "by faith" (*to ek pisteōs*) be referred to the just with this meaning—he who by faith is just—or to life, meaning—the just lives by faith. They amount to the same thing and each is true—that both he who by faith is just, obtains salvation; and again he who is just, obtains salvation by faith. In vain, therefore, is it said that Paul understands a living faith and that it alone is not such, but with works. Although living faith is never alone in the person who is justified, still it is alone in the very act of justification—to the production of which the other virtues can contribute nothing, faith alone claiming this privilege for itself (as we have said before). No better do others wish that life to be referred to the works by which faith proves itself alive. The design of the prophet is to teach that faith alone is the means of obtaining salvation, both temporal and spiritual. And Paul says that this righteousness by faith is manifested without the law; which cannot be said of the righteousness of works, but only of the righteousness of faith; which is aid of the man believing, not of one working.

It is one thing for love and works to be required in the person who is justified (which we grant); another in the act itself or causality of justification (which we deny). If works are required as concomitants of faith, they are not on that account determined to be causes of justification with faith or to do the very thing which faith does in this matter.

Although the whole force of justifying on the part of man is in faith as to the act of apprehension (so that other virtues contribute nothing to it with faith), it does not follow that faith can justify when they are absent as well as when they are present—yea, even when the opposite vices are present. It is one thing to justify without virtues (i.e., separated from them—which we deny); another for it to justify alone, but not separated from them. As it does not follow, the hand alone writes and the eye alone sees—therefore as much when torn from the head and the other members as in the body; the sole force of respiration is in the lungs—therefore the lungs can respire torn out from the liver and other viscera as well as when connected with them (which everyone sees to be absurd). There are hundreds of things of this kind which have a certain proper efficacy and effect, which still, when separated from their adjuncts, lose all their power. Natural potencies are connected as to existence, but disjoined as to operation. Light and heat in the sun are most closely connected together, but still the light alone illuminates, the heat alone warms. Therefore, although the other virtues do not justify with faith, still faith cannot justify in their absence, must less the opposite vices being present. For faith cannot be true except in connection with the virtues (which if they do not contribute to justification, still contribute to the existence and life of faith, which the presence of vices would destroy).

It is one thing for the love of the sinner to be the cause of the remission of sins *a priori;* another to be the effect and proof *a posteriori.* The latter is affirmed in Luke 7:47, not the former. We gather this: (1) from the scope of the parable, which is to demonstrate which of two debtors, whose debt the creditor had cancelled, ought to love the creditor most (to wit, in token of gratitude); (2) from the answer of Peter, "I suppose that he, to whom he forgave most," where love is placed as following, not as going before remission; (3) from the end, where a small remission is put as the cause of a small degree of love, "To whom little is forgiven, the same loveth little" (v. 47); (4) from v. 50, where salvation is ascribed to the faith, not to the love, of this woman, "Thy faith hath saved thee." Nor does the particle *hoti* stand in the way because (as is known) it is so often only ratiocinative, not causal—the cause of the consequent, not of the consequence, so as to intimate that thence is known and gathered that many sins were forgiven her because she loved much.

When John says, "We know that we have passed from death unto life, because we love the brethren" (1 John 3:14), he teaches that love is a proof and sign of our justification from which we know that we have passed from death unto life. For he who is in love is in God (who is love) and he who is in God, cannot be in death. But he does not mean that love is the cause of that translation (which is elsewhere ascribed to faith, John 5:24). Hence Lorinus and Gagnaeus on this passage well remark that "the causal article denotes the cause, not of the thing but of the knowledge." On this account even the more, that since God loved us first (not we God, 1 John 4:10), the justification by which God loved us ought to precede our love.

Christ promises "the love of the Father" to those who love him (John 14:23), not affectively and as to its beginning (as if the love of the Father then begins, since he loved us before, 1 John 4:10), but effectively and as to continuance and increase because he will prove his love by distinguished blessings and console them by a new manifestation of himself. But this has nothing to do with justification because to love Christ and to keep his commands belongs to a man already constituted in grace and justified.

The "fear of the Lord" (to wit, filial and reverential) is a consequence of justification, not a previous disposition to it. It is not called "the beginning of wisdom" (Ps. 111:10) as if it initially disposes to wisdom, but because it is its head and perfection, as it is said to be in Ecc. 12:13, which begins from it (Prov. 9:10) and ends in it. If it is said *apōtheisthai hamartēmata* (Sir. 1:21), this ought not to be understood of a positive expulsion (as if it introduced either meritoriously or dispositively remission of sins), but of a negative expulsion because he who fears God does not indulge in sins, nor give ear to their solicitations.

It is one thing for hope to concur to salvation; another for it to concur to justification. The former is asserted in Romans 5:5 and 8:24 when hope is said not to make us ashamed; yea, also to save us. For the expectation of salvation is founded upon a hope so certain to be fulfilled in its own time, as if we already possessed salvation itself. But not the latter because the object of hope is not the remission of sins, but the fulfillment of the promised salvation.

Although remission of sins is promised to repentance (because it ought to accompany faith and be in him who is justified as a certain condition requisite from him because God cannot pardon sin to an impenitent), it does not follow that it can be said to justify with faith because it contributes nothing (neither meritoriously, nor instrumentally) to the act of justification.

It is one thing for eternal life and the heavenly inheritance to be referred to works as meritorious or instrumental causes of our justification; another as effects of faith and qualities and dispositions requisite in the subject to be glorified. As it is one thing to seek "why" (*quare*) life is given to believers; another "upon what" (*quibus*) or "upon what qualities" (*qualibus*) it depends. The former we deny because our works of whatever kind cannot merit life, nor have they the relation of an instrument for apprehending it. But the latter we grant. Nor is anything different gathered from Matthew 25:34–35, where works are not adduced by the Judge as "the foundations of the right" which they obtain to eternal life. The proper cause of that right is indicated in the preceding verses, when they are called "ye blessed of my Father," who ought "to inherit (*klēronomein*) the kingdom" (i.e., possess it by a title of inheritance). Rather they are adduced as arguments and testimonies indubitable *a posteriori*, from which the truth of their faith could be proved, and the equity of the sentence pronounced (as the particle *gar* is not causal [*aitiologikē*], but only ratiocinative).

Since Paul and James were inspired by the same Spirit, they cannot be said to oppose each other on the doctrine of justification, so that one should ascribe justification to faith alone and the other to works also. The reconciliation is not difficult, if the design of each be considered and the natures of faith and of justification (concerning which both treat) be attended. Paul disputes against the Pharisees, who urged the merits of works; James disputes against the Libertines and Epicureans, who, content with a profession of faith alone, denied not only the merits of works, but also their necessity. Against the former, Paul rightly urges faith alone for justification. Against the latter, James properly commends the necessity of works for the confirmation of justification. Paul speaks of a living and efficacious faith; James of an idle and dead faith which cannot be demonstrated by works (2:19); Paul of justification *a priori* and constitutively; James of the same *a posteriori* and declaratively; Paul properly constitutes the former in faith alone; James rightly places the latter in works, by which the reality of our faith and justification is declared not only before men, but also before God. Therefore, when faith is said "to have wrought with works in Abraham, and by works to have been made perfect" (v. 22), this ought to be understood in relation to the efficacy of faith, which exerted itself by works and by which also it was consummated and made perfect. It ought not to be understood essentially, for this it has by its own nature (but declaratively) because it is proven to be perfect and sincere; just as "the power of God" is said to be "made perfect in our weakness" (2 Cor. 12:9), i.e., known and declared to be perfect.

It is one thing for works to be connected with faith in the person of the justified; another, however, in the matter of justification. The former we acknowledge and will afterwards prove, when we discuss the necessity of good works; but the latter we deny with Paul—nay, we maintain that they are wholly incompatible (*asystata*) with faith.

Augustine says rightly, "Good works do not precede the one to be justified, but follow the one justified." A person is justified freely by faith without works (Rom. 3:24); yea, justification is of the wicked (Rom. 4:5; 5:6). No good works can be granted which precede his justification as causes, but only which follow as the effects and fruits springing from the faith of remission (Luke 7:47; 1 Tim. 1:5). If calling (by which faith and holiness are infused) is prior to justification, it does not follow that holiness no less than faith is prior to it because holiness is indeed infused, but in its own order and by faith (Acts 15:9). Faith however concurs to justification before it does to sanctification. If remission is sometimes promised to repentance, this is indeed promised to it as a condition not antecedent or concomitant by reason of contrition, but only consequent as to new obedience.

# 9

# THE TIME OF JUSTIFICATION

*Was justification made from eternity or is it made in time? Is it an undivided act taking place at one and the same time?*

The opinions of theologians about this question vary. Some maintain that it is an immanent act in God which was performed from eternity; others that it is transient, terminating in us and which takes place only in time and in this life. And there are some who hold that it is postponed to the last and decretory day, in which all must stand before the solemn and public tribunal of Christ to hear the sentence of absolution or of condemnation from his lips. Now although there is an agreement on both sides in the substance of the thing and a disagreement only in the mode of the thing, still it is of no little importance to the accurate knowledge of the subject to know what is the true opinion to be held here.

The first opinion is that of those who hold that justification preceded our birth and was made in eternity because they conceive it to be an immanent and internal act in God.

However, as nothing new can happen to God in time, they think it was made in him from eternity and is ascribed to faith only as to cognizance and sense because it leads us into the knowledge of him and makes us certain of it.

But although we do not deny that our justification was decreed even from eternity (as nothing takes place in time which was not constituted by him from eternity), still we do not think (speaking accurately) justification itself can be called eternal. The decree of justification is one thing; justification itself another—as the will to save and sanctify is one thing; salvation and sanctification itself another. The will or decree to justify certain persons is indeed eternal and precedes faith itself, but actual justification takes place in time and follows faith.

Second, Paul expressly confirms this in the chain of salvation, enumerating in order the benefits flowing to the elect from the eternal love of God where he puts calling before justification as something antecedent: "Whom he called, them he justified" (Rom. 8:30). Nor have those various passages a different meaning in which we are said to be justified through and by faith, than that faith is a something prerequisite to justification. This could not be said if justification was done from eternity. For it is weak and foreign to the meaning of Paul to refer these things to the sense of justification only.

Third, the nature of the thing itself proves this. For since justification or remission of sins necessarily involves a deliverance from the obligation to punishment which sins deserved and no one can obtain it without faith and repentance, it is evident that such a justification could not have been made from eternity, but only in time—when the man actually believes and repents. Otherwise it would follow that he who is justified and consequently has passed from death unto life and become a child of God and an heir of eternal life, still remains in death and is a child of wrath. He who is not yet converted and lies in sin, remains in death (1 John 3:14) and is of the Devil (1 John 3:8) and in a state of condemnation (Gal. 5:21).

Finally, since justification is a blessing of God, while a blessing cannot pass to us and be actually bestowed upon us, except in time, it is clear that it is not to be conceived of after the manner of an immanent and internal act in God, but after the manner of a transient act arising from God and passing over and terminating upon the creature (not that it may subjectively inhere in him, as the Romanists falsely hold because this pertains to sanctification; but that it may adhere to him and the creature has an objective relation to it, while the absolving sentence is intimated to him by the Holy Spirit). If grace is said to have been given to us in Christ before the world began by reason of "destination" (2 Tim. 1:9) because from eternity God decreed to give it to us in time, it does not follow that it can be said to have been really bestowed because the decree indeed causes us to obtain in time a right to life certainly and infallibly, but not that we can say we already obtained it actually. It causes that we should be justified, but not to be already justified.

But as justification cannot be conceived to have taken place from eternity before the ages, so neither ought it to be thrown forward to the consummation of the world as others hold—as if God only then exercises properly the act of a Judge, both in the pardon of believers and in the condemnation of the wicked. For thus the declaration of justification is falsely confounded with justification itself. For although we are told the heavenly Judge will then sit on his throne of the glory to exercise the last solemn act of judgment (as much in grace as in justice, in the sight of heaven and earth), this does not prevent that judgment from commencing in the present life. Nay, this must necessarily be supposed, since that final judgment is nothing else than a public and solemn manifestation of preceding judgments. And as Scripture everywhere sets before us the examples of God's judgments, public as well as private over the wicked and rebellious (such as the flood, the destruction of Sodom, the overthrow of the Egyptians and the like), to refer these to mere chastisements of God, tending towards the improvement and salvation of those upon whom they were sent, is to contradict the whole tenor of Scripture and rashly to confound the medicinal chastisements of believers (which are sent upon them for instruction [*paideian*] by God as a merciful Father) with the punishments of the wicked (which are inflicted by God as an angry Judge, to punish [*timōrian*] and avenge himself of their sins)—which has thus far been unheard-of in theological schools. So that he is evidently a stranger to the Scriptures who does not know that God is often set forth as justifying believers in this life; as is evident from the examples of Abraham (Gen. 15:6), of David (Ps. 32:1–2, 5; Rom. 4:6–7), of the sinful woman (Luke 7:48), of the publican (Luke 18:14) and of all believers (Rom. 5:1). Not to say now that that opinion is hurtful to the consolation of believers, which springs from no other source more certainly than from a sense of the grace of God and his justification. For how else could they have the confidence in which they glory and exult on account of their justification and enjoy unspeakable (*aneklalētō*) peace and joy?

This opinion then being dismissed, we embrace the middle one, which makes justification to take place in this life in the moment of effectual calling, by which the sinner is transferred from a state of sin to a state of grace and is united to Christ, his head, by faith. For hence it is that the righteousness of Christ is imputed to him by God, by whose merit apprehended by faith he is absolved from his sins and obtains a right to life. This absolving sentence, the Spirit pronounces in his heart when he says, "Be of good courage, son, thy sins are pardoned."

Further, this justification can be regarded in different ways: (1) actively on the part of God intimating by the Spirit the absolving sentence in the heart of the believer and judicially from the throne of grace (Heb. 4:16), pronouncing it upon us; and passively on our part, inasmuch as we admit and receive that absolving sentence delivered in the court of conscience by the Holy Spirit with faith, joy and the protestation of gratitude.

Second, universally as to state, when we are first received into union with Christ, and his righteousness is imputed to us by God and received by faith. For then in passing from a state of sin into a state of grace, the guilt of all preceding sins is actually taken away and a remedy given to us in the righteousness of Christ against future sins. And specially as to particular acts of sin into which we afterwards fall, which also need a particular absolution. As often as it is intimated to us in the court of conscience, so often the believer is by repentance turned again to God and by faith applies to himself Christ's righteousness. In this sense, we are commanded to seek remission of sins every day; not only with regard to the sense, but also with regard to the thing itself because sins cannot be forgiven unless committed (as we remarked before).

Third, justification can be viewed in a twofold aspect (*schesei*): either as to the "eternal destination" in the decree, in which sense grace is said "to have been given to us in Christ before the world began" (2 Tim. 1:9) and God is said to have "predestinated us unto the adoption" (Eph. 1:5); or as to its execution in time which again can be regarded on the one hand as to obtainment, which was made by the death of Christ on the cross (referred to in Rom. 5:9–10: "We were justified and reconciled to God by the blood of Christ";

and "Christ reconciled all things to God through the blood of the cross," Col. 1:20). Elsewhere Christ is said to "have been raised again for our justification" (Rom. 4:25) because as in him dead, we are dead, so in him raised and justified, we are justified (i.e., we have a sure and indubitable pledge and foundation of our justification because for no other cause was he justified by the Spirit [1 Tim. 3:16] except that we might be justified in him). Nor in a different sense does Paul say, "God was in Christ, reconciling the world unto himself, not imputing their trespasses unto them" (2 Cor. 5:19); to wit, inasmuch as in Christ dying, the Father had the foundation of reconciliation by which he was made more propitious to the world of the elect, collected as well from the Jews as from the Gentiles, so that he does not impute to them their sins (which he imputed to Christ), but by absolving them from their sins, he may justify them also in him. On the other hand it may be viewed as to application, which is made in the heart by an intimation of the absolving sentence (referred to in Matt. 9:2). Or it may be viewed in general as to the state of the believer when he is first called; or in particular as to the act when he obtains the pardon of particular sins; or as to the sense and certainty of it, arising in us from a reflex act of faith (called consolatory); or finally, as to its declaration, which should be made immediately after death (Heb. 9:27) and publicly on the last day (which is not so much justification, as a solemn declaration of the justification once made and an adjudication of the reward, in accordance with the preceding justification).

Hence it is evident in what sense justification can be called an undivided act; not on our part and with respect to the sense of it (which is produced by various and repeated acts according as this sense can be interrupted; or increased or diminished, by reason of interfering sins); but on the part of God, not only by reason of his decree (by which our justification was decreed) and by reason of his merit (by which he obtained it), but also by reason of the application when the absolving sentence is intimated to us. This is done by a unique act, not by many successive acts, just as inherent righteousness is wont to be infused into us (although this act is often applied to particular everyday sins).

# 10

# THE UNITY OF
# JUSTIFICATION

*The unity, perfection and certainty of justification.*

Unity, perfection and certainty are the three principal adjuncts of justification concerning which disputes exist. Of these we must speak briefly because we have elsewhere discussed them partially.

Unity can be regarded in two ways: either relative to believers among themselves; or absolutely with respect to him who is justified. In the former sense, it is said to be "one in species" or "equal in all believers" of all times and places because God justifies all believers in the same manner (viz., by his grace and the merit of Christ through faith). "Seeing it is one God," says the apostle, "which shall justify the circumcision by faith, and the uncircumcision through faith" (Rom. 3:30), i.e., who justifies the Jews as well as the Gentiles by faith. For since all are liable to sin and condemnation (v. 19), and destitute of the glory of God (v. 23), there is no other method of justification than by faith. The apostle proves this fully in the same place and confirms it by the examples of David and of Abraham (Rom. 4); as also of all the saints of the Old Testament mentioned in Heb. 11, who by faith are said to have pleased God (v. 6), to have obtained witness that they were righteous (v. 4) and to have become heirs of the righteousness which is by faith (v. 7). Nor either in the Old or New Testament can there be found any dissimilar example of a person justified in another way. Hence Peter says, "To him give all the prophets witness, that through his name whosoever believeth in him shall receive remission of sins" (Acts 10:43). Through the grace of Christ, we shall be saved, even as they (Acts 15:11). Christ is the same yesterday, today and forever (Heb. 13:8); he is the Way, and the Truth and the Life; no one can come to the Father except by him (John 14:6).

For the objections brought forward here by the Socinians against the identity of the justification of the believers of the Old and New Testaments, see Topic XII, Question 5 concerning the unity of the covenant of grace (where they are discussed).

Now although the same benefit as to substance was common to the believers of the Old Testament no less than to those of the New (as they had true remission of sins in and on account of Christ), still there was a multiple difference as to degree and sense. It is far more clearly revealed and more fully and efficaciously felt by us now; as was proved in the same place and in Question 12.

Second, the same justification is one numerically in individuals. It is not promoted successively after the manner of sanctification by repeated acts, but is finished in one judicial act and brings to the believer the remission of all sins. Hence the Romanists (from their fictitious hypothesis concerning physical justification by an infusion of righteousness) falsely make it twofold: the first, that by which a man from being unjust is made just by an infusion of righteousness; the second, that by which from being just he is made more just by the increase of righteousness. The foundation having been once overturned (as was done above), whatever is built upon it falls. Nor does the passage in Revelation 22:11 favor this error because (as we have already said), it does not treat of the infusion of righteousness, but either of the sense and declaration of righteousness once gained (which is retained by the exercise of righteousness) or of its special application to everyday sins.

The distinction between active and passive justification points out indeed the truth of the terms "from which" and "to which" (viz., of God who justifies and of man who is justified), but does not change the degree or species. For by the same sentence by which God justifies us (while he intimates it to the conscience), we are also passively justified when it is received by us through faith.

The blessing of justification and the right to it differ from the feeling and the knowledge of it. There is no cutting off or renewal of the former because it is a gift without repentance (*ametamelēton*). The latter, however, may be interrupted and restored according to the various increases and decreases of sanctification. And although that sense may be interrupted in grievous sins and be recovered by various and repeated acts, still the blessing of justification remains always in him the same.

Although our justification will be fully declared on the last day (our good works also being brought forward as the sign and proof of its truth, Matt. 25:34–40), still falsely would anyone maintain from this a twofold gospel justification— one from faith in this life (which is the first); the other (and second) from works on the day of judgment (as some hold, agreeing too much with Romanists on this point). The sentence to be pronounced by the supreme Judge will not be so much a new justification, as the solemn and public declaration of a sentence once passed and its execution by the assignment of the life promised with respect to an innocent person from the preceding justification. Thus it is nothing else than an adjudicatory sentence of the possession of the kingdom of heaven from the right given before through justification. And if works are then brought forward, they are not adduced as the foundation of a new justification to be obtained then, but as signs, marks and effects of our true faith and of our justification solely by it.

It is one thing to apply justification often and to extend it to sins of daily occurrence (in which sense we are commanded to seek remission of sins every day); another to repeat and renew justification often. The former we grant, but not the latter. Nor is there need that a new justification should take place as often as the believer falls into a new sin. It is sufficient that the justification once made (which if not formally, virtually and generically contains the remission of all sins) be applied and extended specifically and determinatively to this or that sin by an intimation of the Holy Spirit and the apprehension of faith.

Although remission of sins ought to be applied often to daily sins, yet falsely would anyone thence gather that sins once discharged revive and return again by subsequent sins (as some of the Romanists hold), since it is an unchangeable (*ametamelēton*) gift of God. Nor does the parable of that ungrateful servant (who, after a greater amount had been yielded to him by his master, wished to deal cruelly with his fellow servant who owed him far less and who on that account was delivered to the tormentors till he should pay all that was due unto him [which is recorded in Matt. 18:23–35]) prove this. It pertains to nothing else than to show that the remission of sins proposed conditionally does not belong to him in whom the condition is lacking. The design of the parable (which is to be regarded here simply) is no other than to teach that the mercy of God is not exercised towards the unmerciful; nor are sins pardoned by God, except to those who forgive the offenses of others. To show this the more efficaciously, the master is opposed here to his servant, an immense sum to a minute and the highest clemency to extreme inhumanity.

(2) Perfection belongs to justification, according to which it is so full and absolute intensively (both with respect to evils taken away and blessings acquired) that it is free as to itself from increase and decrease. Nor does it admit of more and less, although as to the apprehension and sense of it our faith advances so gradually as to have even its progressions and defects. If the faith by which we are justified is active and remitted, it does not follow that justification itself is equally intermittent because it does not justify by itself and properly, but only instrumentally and relatively; as the beholding of the brazen serpent did not cease equally to heal, although some looked at it more intently and strongly than others.

(3) Its certainty is twofold: one of the object in itself by the immutability and perseverance by which God never recalls the pardon once given (on account of the immutability of his grace, justice and promise confirmed by an oath, Heb. 6:17–18). For the gifts of God bestowed upon the elect and the calling according to his purpose (*kata prothesin*) are without repentance (*ametamelēta*, Rom. 11:29). Hence God never condemns and disinherits those whom he has once justified and made heirs. The other is the certainty of the subject, which refers to the sense of justification. Although it is possible from the nature of faith (yea, even necessary to bring peace and consolation to our souls), still it is not always in the same degree—but more perfect or imperfect according to the proportion of faith, so that there never was a believer (not even excepting Abraham [Gen. 17:17], or David [Ps. 42:5, 11]) who did not have to struggle with doubts concerning grace. How each of these certainties belong to justification has already been shown fully, when we discussed the perseverance and certainty of faith; cf. Topic XV, Questions 16 and 17.

# INDEX OF SCRIPTURE